The Pocket Adoption Coach

Wisdom for life shared through heartening personal account

MICHELE HENGEN
ASSOCIATE CERTIFIED COACH

 FriesenPress

Suite 300 - 990 Fort St
Victoria, BC, V8V 3K2
Canada

www.friesenpress.com

ISBN
978-1-03-910031-2 (Hardcover)
978-1-03-910030-5 (Paperback)
978-1-03-910032-9 (eBook)

1. Family & Relationships, Adoption & Fostering

Distributed to the trade by The Ingram Book Company

Dedicated to Katja, Matt and Nick

You grew not under my heart but in it.
You are such blessings in our lives and I am
forever grateful to be your Mom.

Thank you also to Dave, who willingly chose to
live out this incredible journey with me. I love the
life and family we have created together.

Contents

PART ONE
General Adoption Topics

Background – Our Story

The Decision Process

The Home Study & Other Documents

Dealing with Reactions of Others

Attachment

Chapter One

Our Story

The first trimester had passed without incident and the initial ultrasound results were promising. However, as I lay in bed that night, I could sense that something wasn't right. I yelled to Dave, stirring him from a comfortable slumber, and cried that I needed to go to the hospital. We wasted no time seeking immediate medical attention. Since our hospital arrival inconveniently occurred early on a Sunday morning, the receptionist was forced to page a doctor at home. I dreaded what the doctor would say while trying to think positive thoughts as I lay waiting in the sterile surroundings of the Swiss hospital. Meanwhile, I couldn't believe this was happening. After all we had gone through, were our dreams going to be taken away? How could that be? We had planned everything right up to this seemingly right time to begin our family. I passed the time reflecting on the events that had brought us to that point.

When Dave and I married on May 7, 1994, we started out as a typical dual-income, healthy, professional couple. We fully expected to naturally bear children as soon as we decided to slot it into our well-orchestrated schedules. In the meantime, we enjoyed the various freedoms available only to the childless, including spontaneous movie nights at a real movie theatre as opposed to watching a rental from the sofa, dinners with more than three courses not including ketchup, and driving in a clean vehicle without a wet cloth in sight.

We had both been born, raised, and educated in Western Canada. Even before we met, we had independently pursued an interest in experiencing what the world had to offer. This alignment proved to be important, as Dave was offered a position in Switzerland early in our married life. After a brief deliberation, we decided we were up for the challenge of an international experience. We packed up our furniture and belongings and we moved overseas.

There, Dave and I thoroughly engrossed ourselves in our new surroundings. We enjoyed over two years of work and travel in another continent, and not necessarily in that order. This experience challenged us two unilingual, North American flatlanders. Once we got used to the lack of such conveniences as neighbourhood dry cleaners and affordable take-out food, we settled into a lovely life of eating Gruyère cheese while gazing at the beautiful, snow-capped Alps. More than merely offering us an opportunity to discover the art of grocery shopping and paying bills in a foreign land, our overseas adventure would play a key role in our development as individuals and as a couple. Unbeknownst to us at the time, contacts we made in Switzerland would profoundly impact the future of our family.

Early in our Swiss experience, we were seeking a new church family, and in the process, stumbled across Westlake Church, which was just around the corner from our apartment. Westlake turned out to be a sanctuary away from home that also led us to some important players in our lives, particularly with respect to our adoption story. Through these contacts, we met a remarkable English missionary, Vic Jackopson. In his role as executive director of the international ministry Hope Now, Vic spearheaded many spectacular works with orphanages and prisons in Ukraine. The tireless Hope Now staff donates time and resources to breathe life into the lives of the children in these otherwise dreary institutions.

We were privileged to experience Vic's engaging personality first-hand, as he occasionally visited Westlake as a guest speaker and was accompanied by his lovely wife and partner, Sue. He would speak passionately about his many international missions, including those in Ukraine. At this time, Hope Now's ministry in Ukraine centred around the city of Cherkasy, approximately 200 kilometres south of Kiev.

During our sojourn in Switzerland, another couple from Westlake successfully adopted a baby girl from one of the Cherkasy orphanages Vic and Sue supported, fittingly called The House of Babies. We joyfully congratulated them when they brought their new daughter home. Beyond that, I paid little attention to the details regarding their adoption proceedings, as I was too consumed with planning our own conception. At this time, adoption was an option that still flew below my radar.

As the topic of attempting a biological family can fill an entire chapter (see Chapter Two), allow me to fast-forward a bit so I can give you an overview of our story upfront. After our experience of postcard-worthy living and working abroad, Dave accepted a transfer back to our home country. This time, we were shipping out to Montreal. This move excited me for many reasons, not the least of which was the closer proximity to family and friends. Family support would become especially important, as our prayers had finally been answered. We were going to have a baby!

We were delighted beyond words. Due to this exciting turn of events, I elected not to take a transfer with the consulting firm that employed me in Switzerland. Although Montreal offered considerable opportunities for my career, I chose to make a full-time transition into my new profession of Motherhood at home, with our yet-to-be-born perfect baby.

Well, since this is a book about adoption, you may wonder whether this pregnancy was meant to be. Let me spare you the suspense. Three days before our move to Montreal, we suffered a miscarriage. All of a sudden, I had no idea what my new life would offer. No job and no baby. What would I do? It was a scary thought. In the short term, the transition may have been smoother had I seamlessly transferred to my firm's Montreal office, which would have been the logical plan if I was not pregnant. Then we could have resumed our comfortable life as a professional working couple trying to stroke *start a family* off our to-do list. But then that miscarriage had to ruin everything. Or did it?

One remarkable human trait is the ability to clearly see the important links between various life events, but only after their effects have all been realized. For example, I misled you in the last paragraph by insinuating that my pregnancy, and even the miscarriage, were not meant to be. Both events played pivotal roles in the development of our family. The pregnancy prevented me from engrossing myself in an instant job upon our arrival in Montreal. The ensuing miscarriage intensified the motivation required to fuel the long journey we had ahead of us in forming our family.

Even though downtown Montreal offers endless choices of nighttime activities, nothing could distract me from yearning for a baby. Each month that pregnancy eluded us, I lapsed into a temporary funk. Having lived a charmed and well-planned existence to that point, I could not understand why this event, which was supposed to be natural, was not at all natural for us. As is the case with many couples in this situation, my partner was much more patient in our baby-making process. Perhaps the potential father is able to enjoy the "process" part while the wannabe mom is more focused on the "baby-making" component. Little did I know that each layer of disappointment would provide me with another round of artillery in our adoption battle. As your Coach, please let me explain by way of a story.

Have you ever witnessed a chick hatch from an egg? Well, this city girl has not, but I have been told that it is a painful experience to watch. The baby chick pecks away from inside the shell for what seems like an eternity and does not appear to make any progress. Apparently, the sight could motivate a kind-hearted spectator to break the shell open so the poor chick could begin its first flight. But this would not help the chick. Such assistance would likely kill it, because the strength gained from breaking through the shell becomes the strength needed to survive outside the shell. Without the opportunity to prepare itself in the safety of the egg, the chick would become instant, helpless fodder for hungry prey.

Similarly, we had to keep pecking away at our attempts to start a family so that our adoption dreams would one day hatch successfully. Without enduring a series of disappointments leading up to our adoptions, we may not have had the fortitude to fight the battles ahead. Unfortunately, this was one of those epiphanies that only became clear much later and after our prayers and efforts had paid off in the form of three wonderful children. Oh, and a few nights of uninterrupted sleep also helped to clarify the situation.

During the months prior to our first adoption, I was completely oblivious to the fact that I was donning my first layers of armour. Each month without a pregnancy, I inched closer to initiating the first steps toward adoption. This gradual progression was not an abrupt conscious decision, but instead was more of a thought evolution. In my mind, I pretended I was in control of the situation by setting an internal deadline. If we didn't achieve pregnancy the very next month, I told myself I would casually float the word "adoption" to Dave, to see how he responded. I played this mind game with myself for several months, until I reached my limit and could wait no longer to test the waters.

A mixture of relief and anxiety rushed through me when Dave said he was open to further investigation. Although we had moved an ocean away, the memory of Vic and Sue Jackopson and the Ukrainian orphanages remained vivid in our minds. I placed a tentative call to Vic in the UK. Imagine our surprise when we received his congratulatory email the very next day regarding our decision to adopt one of the children supported through Hope Now! He was much quicker than we were to commit to this path. We were initially concerned that we could be setting ourselves up for a big disappointment if all did not go according to plan. But once we did commit to adoption, we approached it with real tenacity and determination to realize our dreams. At no time were we ever guaranteed that the adoption would reach fruition. In fact, we would encounter several roadblocks in the coming months that at times seemed insurmountable.

I will share the complete story of how we officially became parents to Katja in March of 1998 in the next section of this book, along with the heartbreaking reason we had to leave her behind in the orphanage and return to Canada without her. After adopting our new daughter, one full month—an eternity—would elapse before we could return to Ukraine to bring her home with us. And then a mere six months after this second and final trip to Ukraine, we were presented with the prospect of another adoption. This time, we had the opportunity to adopt an infant locally, who was yet to be born to a brave young girl. As it turned out, this gestating baby would multiply into twins, and so, on May 27, 1999, Matthew and Nicholas joined our family. Our second (and third!) adoption experiences differed significantly from our first, as you will discover in the pages ahead. But the end result was the same, as our family was blessed with the addition of two more precious lives. We had never been so rich—or busy!

Before I share these unique stories and the lessons to be gleaned from them, I want to introduce some coaching advice that is applicable to the vast majority of adoptions. Here it is: it is important to keep the end goal in mind and not let anyone or anything get in your way. Stay true to your feeling that this is the right path for you. For a variety of reasons, prospective adoptive parents may meet resistance at various points. Just because something has never been done before doesn't mean it can't be done, providing it's legal, ethical and moral. So, you may need to stand your ground as you pave a few paths. Additionally, reaching your family goals often calls for some significant innovative thinking. Keep reminding yourself of the child who will join your family. Along the way you will connect with people in ways you cannot imagine, and you might acquire some skills that are relevant to your personal and professional lives, as I did. Allow me to explain what I mean at a high level and then I will reinforce these concepts throughout the pages ahead.

Everyone with whom I share our adoption experiences marvels at our extraordinary luck. I do not contradict them, as I do feel extremely fortunate and grateful for the beautiful family we created. But this reaction conjures up difficult memories of the months of dedication and effort that led to our successes, during which I felt like the *unluckiest* person in the world. I still need to pinch myself to believe that, within only fourteen months, we managed to acquire not one, not two, but three healthy and beautiful children. The plan for our lives was much bigger than I could have ever imagined. Remembering this experience continues to come in handy whenever I'm frustrated that my plans do not seem to be unfolding as I think they should.

Even with miracles sprinkled in with our plans, we needed to do our part to complete our adoptions, and that meant injecting a healthy dose of stubbornness and pride into the process. At several junctures in our path, third parties informed us that what we planned to do could not possibly be accomplished. Had we believed them, all five of our lives would have turned out drastically differently.

For example, it did not take long to discover that there were no adoption agencies in Quebec that dealt with Ukraine. The solution presented was to simply pick another country. But it wasn't so simple of a solution for us, given that we had, at this point, already been introduced to Katja through photos and letters. Switching to another country of adoption was no more viable an option than switching babies in the hospital would be for a birth mother. Eventually, I established with the Quebec government that, with or without their help, we would be adopting a child from Ukraine. I was pleased to receive their positive encouragement. At the same time, they could not provide any practical guidance, as they had no precedence for our unique situation.

Further complicating our plan was the fact that, by pre-selecting Katja, we were opposing official Ukrainian rules. The Ukraine law required that adoptive parents first receive federal and local permission to adopt a child; only then are they privy to review the government files of select children open to adoption. We did not believe the rules would have to preclude us from adopting

Katja, with whom we had already connected through pictures and reports from Hope Now.

Our efforts paid off and the Ukrainian courts declared us the legal parents of Katja. But the saga did not stop there, as we were once again told we could not bring our daughter home with us. This time, we could not blame the Ukrainians. We only had our own government to blame, as it had denied our request for the proper immigration papers to bring our daughter into our own country. At several bureaucratic levels, the message came through that there was nothing we could do to change the course of events. As discussed in Chapter Nine, we refused to listen and, after a grueling month of lobbying, we were given special permissions to finally bring our daughter home. Two days later, Dave and I boarded another plane to do so.

We were better prepared for our second adoption. The complicating factor in this case was that Quebecois birth mothers did not have the legal right to decide where their unborn babies would be placed. As soon as a birth mother announced her intention to give her baby up for adoption, she relinquished all control and the government intervened in placing the baby with a family. As far as we know, Quebec was the only jurisdiction in North America in which this was the case. So, how could we legally become the adoptive parents of these unborn twins?

Once again, we heard the all-too-familiar words: "You can't do that!" By now, we had enough proof to disregard these discouraging words, as long as we maintained enough inspiration to realize our family dreams. They were too vivid for us to give up merely because our plan did not fit into the normal procedure manual. The importance of developing a clear vision and holding onto it is a life lesson that was key to our adoption success, and one that I will reinforce through this book.

And so it happened that, after a rocky start to our family-building efforts, we were blessed with our three children. I firmly believe the good fortune we experienced and skills we developed are available to others, provided the potential parents feel confident about realizing their dreams. Otherwise, your motivation may wane as cynics cast doubts on your plans. There may be times you need to tune out when others say your dreams are not possible, even if their words come from the most well-intentioned sources. The encouragement you need at these times may be difficult to find, unless someone in your inner circle has personal adoption experience. And without a personal support group to rely on, you might seek comforting information from a book or, in a pinch, my personal favourite therapist, Dr. Google.

Compared to other similarly poignant subjects, adoption has been sorely neglected on the real and virtual bookshelves. I did not know this until I sought the same genre of book that had comforted me throughout our quest to conceive, and then through my twelve weeks of pregnancy. At that time, I was amazed to discover the multitude of shelves devoted exclusively to the topics of conception, pregnancy, and childbirth. Each subject on its own constituted a fertile breeding ground for books. Not only did the volume of books impress me, but so did their diversity of topics. I bought everything, from factual medical books to humorous self-help books. After miscarrying a few days before our move to Montreal, I just had enough time to cram them all into boxes, as I no longer had a need for them.

By the time I unpacked the books at the other end of our move, we were considering the adoption option. Revisiting the pages of these pregnancy-related books reminded me of the consolation they provided throughout a very trying time. Naively, I trotted off to the neighbourhood bookstore to search for similar books on the subject of adoption, but I was disheartened when I could not uncover the same source of comfort that I had found in the pregnancy section months before.

Still undeterred, I set off to the largest English bookstore in downtown Montreal to research my topic. Once I was within the walls of the four-level bookstore, my first destination was the family and childcare section. While wading through the sea of hardcovers and paperbacks, including the newly arrived *Complete Guide to Surviving Week 32 of Pregnancy* and *Breastfeeding During a Full Moon* books, I was hopeful I would find one little book devoted to the topic of adoption. But nothing jumped out at me. I decided to ask for help.

In the distance, I spotted a bookstore employee sorting through the various childbirth books and, believing he would be an expert on any topic related to family expansion, I picked up one of my favourite pregnancy-related books and asked for something similar in the adoption section. By his skeptical expression, I realized I might as well have been asking for the *1001 Things for a Mother to Do in her Spare Time* section. He even went so far as to suggest I was picky in my choice of topics! After I repeated my request for any related books, he intimated that perhaps I would find something in the legal section. I could only imagine how humorous and reader-friendly those might be.

It became clear that it would be easier to write the type of book I needed than to buy one. Which brings us here. In the process, if I can help one individual or couple visualize an adoption in their future, this book will have accomplished its mission. You see, like marriage, an adoption requires an active decision-making process. In this way, adoption may differ from a natural childbirth. Have you ever heard about an unplanned or accidental adoption? This could never happen, because at each stage of progression, the adoptive parents must actively choose to advance to the next phase. Complicating the decision is that each new step is more invasive and expensive than the last.

Just as a hurdler focuses on the finish line, I want potential adoptive parents to focus on the child who could be awaiting them at this very moment. Once the decision to adopt becomes a firm commitment, the opposition or hardships faced are just a little easier to clear. By sharing the circumstances of our hurdles and subsequent successes throughout the following pages, I hope you or someone you know will be able to move closer to completing a beautiful family.

Chapter Two

Grounds for Adoption

P arents are not typically expected to state their motives for bearing children. After all, who could possibly question a process that comes about so naturally? On the other hand, some presume that adoptive parents only default to this option as a last resort. In some cases, this may be true, but that in no way relegates adoption to a less desirable option. Many parents voluntarily pursue adoption from the outset. And no matter which motivating factor leads to an eventual adoption, the outcome is just as miraculous as if the adoptive parents physically created the baby themselves.

Adoption can be a beautiful means to creating a loving family. It is crucial that those pursuing an adoption remain focused on their own personal and unique primary motivating factors as they encounter pesky obstacles that may arise during the process. Along that vein, this entire chapter is devoted to exploring a few of the more common adoption catalysts.

Motivation #1—Infertility

Notwithstanding the introduction to this chapter, no comprehensive adoption book would be complete without a section devoted to a key factor leading to many adoptions: infertility. Technically, infertility is defined as a lack of pregnancy after trying for twelve months, while sterility refers to the grim diagnosis that pregnancy is impossible. The good news is that most causes of infertility can be overcome. The bad news is that few dignities remain when a couple undergoes several rounds of fertility testing. Both parties are poked and prodded to determine their value as breeding stock. Intimate details become scientific facts within the procreation project. And even after experiencing several setbacks, there is no guarantee of success.

If you are one of the lucky souls who cannot personally relate to this section, then hopefully you will at least gain a little sympathy for others who can. Certainly, I never realized just how many people struggle with this issue until I began to investigate the subject. I was told once that approximately fifteen percent of all couples in North America are classified as infertile.

If you think we have a harder time of it than our parents did, you are right. The primary reason for this is simple. Women today are trying to get pregnant at a later age than their mothers and grandmothers did. Our society has evolved such that the average age of women having children has increased by up to three years over the last few decades. Until someone discovers the fountain of youth, it is an indisputable fact that fertility rates decline with age. But don't let this discourage you too much. Just take comfort in the knowledge that it is supposed to take longer to conceive if you are over twenty-five. If you are voluntarily reading this book for your own purposes, you may already be in that category.

As we started our family-building project when I was twenty-nine, I was acutely aware of the fertility rate scales. Statistics may vary, but all sources seem to agree on one fact: there is a noticeable drop in fertility after age thirty. I was reminded of this detail every time the type of medical article I tried to avoid kept jumping out at me from nowhere in big, bold letters: *Fertility Rates Plunge after Thirty*. The literature had me convinced that if I did not get pregnant by my thirtieth birthday, we might as well forget about trying.

My advice to you is to read nothing but *Popular Mechanics* or *Better Homes and Gardens* at all times throughout your baby-making project. Do not be drawn into enticing websites or magazine covers that lead you to believe that the words within will not smack you with discouraging facts. I recall leafing through a financial magazine in the doctor's office as I thought it would be safe. But even this innocent-looking journal contained an article heralding the success of some new product that would apparently reverse infertility rates. A significant portion of the article was devoted to outlining the bleakest of bleak statistics. I knew then that nothing was safe. There was nowhere to hide from this cloud of negative information.

To save you the trauma of reading these doom-and-gloom articles, I will pass on some of the facts that may actually be helpful in your situation. As stated previously, the reality is that infertility rates *do* steadily decrease after age twenty-five, and more rapidly after the age of thirty. If this were a medical journal, this would be a good time to break out fancy graphs highlighting the exponential growth of the infertility rate as a function of age. Don't worry, though, because unless you've been diagnosed as infertile, the chances of pregnancy are greater than zero. Unfortunately, sometimes, that is not enough.

My mother never concerned herself with these statistics, as

she married at the tender age of nineteen to my father, who was a mere twenty-three. Approximately two percent of nineteen-year-old women are infertile. By the time my mother was twenty-five, she had four children. At age twenty-five, I had not even met my husband. Where was he when my fertility was peaking?

Some couples are fortunate enough to conceive their first child quickly, but then are subsequently disappointed to discover that a sibling does not follow so easily. There is even an appropriately named clinical term for this occurrence: secondary infertility. This is where the concept of averages becomes difficult in real life. What the statistics fail to point out is an average can be calculated with many small numbers and many large numbers in the mix. Couples experiencing secondary infertility are just doing their part to contribute to the societal average of time to conception.

A lesser-known phenomenon prevails in Western civilizations. Regardless of age, overall fertility rates in the Western world have been dropping steadily. Although experts do not always agree on why this is occurring, one factor is that average sperm counts have not only decreased but the ones that remain are less talented swimmers. Some studies indicate up to a 60 percent decrease in sperm counts over the last few decades. Like me, you might question how many are really needed, since it only takes one little fighter to swim upstream and fertilize the egg. I mean, millions of chances per millilitre sound like pretty good odds, even for this skeptical statistician. However, according to the fertility experts, this drop has had a dramatic effect on conception rates.

Popular misconceptions might lead us to blame the would-be-father for the sperm reduction he caused due to the skin-tight jeans he wore in his earlier years. Perhaps there is some minute truth to this. Of more relevance is the tightness of his jeans today, as any slight rise in temperature can kill those precious sperm. I read a humorous and true story about a truck driver who nestled an ice pack on his lap during his travels. He sought to mitigate the reduction in his sperm count that might have resulted from sitting in his cramped seat all day. No matter what measures a man takes to increase his sperm count, the main culprit is not so easily reversed. The environment—specifically, chemicals and other pollutants in the air—is considered a key source of reduced sperm counts in Western countries.

I do not wish to demoralize anyone, so suffice it to say that all signs indicate infertility is on the rise. The good news to reiterate is that you are not alone if you are experiencing this situation. More importantly, success stories of fertility-challenged couples willing to tolerate—and underwrite—the actions required to bear a child are easily found. A wealth of information including step-by-step procedures on how to beat the odds is readily available through credible medical sources. On a personal level, I found the most inspiring information during our baby-making project came from the true stories of real people who had not only endured infertility but triumphed over it. For some, a triumph means a long-awaited pregnancy. For others, it may come in a different package. What is consistent is that the time between starting to try to get pregnant and wrapping up the baby project can seem tortuous.

As a side note, I have to state that the word '*try*' in this context is one of my pet peeves. Why does the conventional term for starting a family have to harbour such negative connotations? One tries to pass an exam or win an election, not to have a child. It can actually be a harmful term for some as it insinuates that those who are not able to get pregnant just didn't try hard enough. Still, society tends to be fond of this expression, and as soon as you tell someone you are trying, your audience really knows what is going on—so why not just confess the truth? And speaking of confessions . . .

I developed an addiction . . . to pregnancy tests

This seems like a good time to admit to you that I had a problem. Monthly trips to the drugstore resulted in the purchase of several different brands of pregnancy tests, just in case one brand was malfunctioning. I took the first test about four days before my cycle was due, and then every six hours until I knew we had to wait for better luck the next month. At first, it was exciting to imagine that this was the month when the little blue line might actually appear. But after several months, and especially following the miscarriage, the distress these little bad news bearers inflicted became so intolerable that at one point, I went off them completely. That was it–I quit cold turkey. There is really no other way to do it. If you try to fool yourself that you will only take one *this month*, what do you do when it comes back negative? You determine that of course there must be some mistake with the test, and so you buy a few more to find out.

Does this sound familiar? As your Coach, I hope that you can learn from my story, as the pharmaceutical companies made a small fortune off me. I can't blame them entirely, as I made the conscious decision to spend money month after month, just to make myself feel sad and discouraged. I found it ironic that women all over the world took these pregnancy tests while hoping for negative results when I was so desperately praying for the opposite.

Considering my obsession with and dependence on the tests, it is quite surprising that my first-ever positive test almost went unnoticed. I was in our Swiss apartment on a Friday, preparing for my parents' impending visit the next day, when, like clockwork, I subjected myself to another round of tests. After several minutes peering through a magnifying glass at the indicator window, I had to admit that there was no little blue line to be found. So, once again, I wrapped up the wand and threw it away. At this point, I was so far gone I did not even want Dave to know about all of the tests I took for fear he would have me banned from the pharmacy. I knew I had a problem but justified my behaviour in the name of the Family Cause.

But on this day, for some unexplained reason, I felt compelled to retrieve the test from the garbage for careful re-examination. I dug it out from under the coffee grounds and held the magic wand up to the window, my squinting eyes trying desperately to see even a shadow of a line. Sure enough, there *was* a little blue line after all. To this day, I do not understand why my subconscious sensed it while my eyes did not see it the first time. Who cared though? I had my first little blue line!

I could hardly wait for Dave to get home to celebrate the news. Imagine my relief and excitement when a second pair of human eyes confirmed my suspicions. I was pregnant! However, Dave was not as excited as me. He felt the results were not significant because the line was so faint. I had to excuse him, as he was not nearly as well-read on the subject as I was at that point. I knew, as do all pregnancy test junkies, that during the very early stages, a faint little line was all it took. Even so, I purchased and took several more tests to confirm the confirmation.

Not content to rest on the laurels of the positive test, I paid close attention to any physical signs of pregnancy. For example, it is common knowledge that sore breasts can be a sign of the condition. I so wanted to experience this symptom that I pounded my chest every month, hoping to discover pain somewhere. Perhaps it was my mind playing tricks on me, but I did feel this pain every month! It was only after I looked back objectively that it occurred to me that the pain was self-inflicted. I also wanted morning sickness in the worst way. More than once I was able to talk myself into such a state of nausea. Speaking of nausea, that reminds me of another unpleasant experience during this time.

In order to prepare for the potential conception, a woman is required to keep her body continually ready and healthy for a pregnancy. The worst part for me was the daily folic acid tablet. I refuse to believe that these tablets need to be the size of a Brussels sprout. My theory is that a vitamin's size is supposed to justify its exorbitant price. But, like millions of other women, I choked down that smelly gargantuan pill every day to ensure our baby had the best opportunity to be healthy.

Fertility testing

Opinions vary as to when it is appropriate for a couple to initiate fertility testing. No other person—not even the staunchest members in your support group—is qualified to make that decision for you and your partner. Everyone has different thresholds around when they feel they need outside help to give nature a bit of a boost. I will warn you that many doctors will not take you seriously until you have been trying to conceive for at least one year. That does not mean you cannot start the testing, but you may be put on the slow track at the beginning.

We made a choice to investigate the procedures before we reached the point of desperation. I do not even remember the conscious decision to be at our first diagnostic appointment, but we somehow found ourselves inside a fertility clinic in Montreal, freely submitting to Round One. This is one of the few times, if not the only time, that the male half of the partnership deserves sympathy. Women endure only minor discomforts, such as doctors blowing up their tiny, fragile fallopian tubes to check for blockage.

Men, on the other hand, have a really painful task. At some point, they will be required to supply a sperm sample and hand it over to the lab technician.

If you have not experienced this first-hand, you can imagine it is a tough assignment for a male. First, the hospital laboratory distributes a large test tube with a capacity of seventy millilitres. The man who does not know that the average sperm sample is only two millilitres feels inadequate with his measly deposit. It does not help when the lab technician asks if there was any spillage. The male ego may take over as he is left to wonder if the previous subjects were able to leave more substantial deposits.

If applicable to your situation, I suggest you make every effort to accompany your partner to the laboratory when he delivers his sample. Your mate may feel particularly squeamish about handing his sample over to a stranger, and your presence can help justify why he is carrying two millilitres of recently released sperm tucked under his arm. If nothing else, there are few amusing moments during fertility testing and so you do not want to miss out on this opportunity. Neither the lab technician nor your partner will directly acknowledge the sample left behind, as if by not discussing it, we all pretend not to know what's in the mystery test tube.

By the time we received the results of our first round of fertility tests, we were already registering quite high on the stress scale. But we survived it. We went through this phase just to learn that all of our respective parts seemed to function properly; we were just diagnosed with bad luck. I could see Dave's chest pump with pride as the doctor gave glowing reports about his millions of little contributions to the process. Not to be outdone, I learned you could set a watch to my ovulation cycle. You would think that this good news would have reassured us, but it left me wondering why we were not having success. As our emotions oscillated between relief and frustration, our hearts sank as we were informed about Round Two.

Dave was discouraged to learn that the doctor wanted another sample. I thought I was comforting him when I noted that it could have been another blood test instead. I think that was about the time he passed out. Meanwhile, my biggest fear came true. Everybody had warned me about that test to which I previously alluded, which was designed to check for blockage in the fallopian tubes. Without going into excruciating detail of what these sadists wanted to do to me, suffice it to say that it involved shooting dye into the sensitive microscopic tubes. On a normal day, my pain tolerance is average for a female, placing it leaps and bounds above that of a warrior male. But I still balked at this test. I consoled myself to some degree knowing that Dave was fighting his own internal battle in conquering the test assigned to him.

In the end, we were very mature about it as we made an "I'll do it if you do it" pact. We prayed for conception more than ever in the month leading up to our tests, so we would be rescued from their discomforts and indignities. But it was not meant to be. And then we managed to put the tests off for a few months before conveniently forgetting about them completely. We somehow lost Dave's sample receptacle and the requisition for my test must have been misfiled somewhere. I guess you could say that we passively decided to let nature take its course for the time being. Also, by this point we had started off on the adoption path. We could always resume the tests if we changed our minds or if we did not have success with alternative options.

We have all heard accounts of people who have endured way more than we did in their fertility testing. Along with the physical and financial pain comes the emotional turbulence that often accompanies the process. I have the utmost sympathy for anyone stuck on this roller coaster.

As they say, the truth is often stranger than fiction, and that is how I felt at times when I worked on this book. For example, as I was reworking my first draft about these sperm samples and other infertility tests, Dave was upstairs recuperating from his, as the laboratory form so clinically labelled it, sterilization procedure. Here I was recounting our struggles to have children while in the throes of preventing more. We had come full circle.

Sharing with the world

No matter how far you are willing to delve into the process, at some point you will be tempted to tell the world about your family expansion plans. If this involves some degree of fertility testing, I will give you a word of caution: not everyone will seem under-standing and supportive. Some people may think you are starting fertility testing too early; others may say you're just over-stressed and need a vacation.

Ultimately, you will hear every story, each one with some grain of truth, about some nameless couple who thought they were infertile but now have the perfect family. If you have already con-vinced yourself that you are the only couple not destined for this happy ending, these well-intentioned messages delivered to bring you hope may instead magnify your frustrations.

If you decide to go public, be prepared to provide frequent progress reports. Resist the temptation to respond to the "How is it going?" questions with replies like "You will be one of the first hundred to know." You may want to have your own appropriate response ready at hand. Dave liked to retort, "There are literally thousands of times that we have tried but have not gotten anything!" If you decide to go ahead and announce your plans to the world, I promise not to respond with an "I told you so." That would make me a hypocrite, as I sent out a massive mailing announcement stating our intentions to begin a family. I fully understood why people wondered what was happening months, and even years, later.

Now that you have announced your plans to trade in your sports car for an SUV, and you have willingly subjected yourself to this trendy form of torture called fertility testing, at some point you will receive results. After checking everything from hormones to blockages, the doctors may have found a plausible reason why pregnancy has eluded you. This is typically good news, as the vast majority of infertility cases are treatable. Or you may find out that nothing is wrong and that you're just contributing additional data to reaffirm society's average amount of time to conceive.

Not all stories have a fairy-tale ending. We all know someone who would be a perfect parent (assuming, of course, that parental perfection was attainable) and who desperately wants children. For reasons beyond our mere human comprehension, some of these people receive the unfortunate news that, short of a miracle, a natural pregnancy will not be possible for them. After a period of mourning and often anger, some may choose to build a very fulfilling life without children. Or they may choose to build their family through other means.

Few events highlight the unfairness of life like the wide variation of experiences singles and couples go through in their quest to have a family. Even now, after all my maternal needs have been met, I still marvel that some couples we met appeared to experience instant-mix pregnancies, while others continue to endure pain and heartbreak to this day with no guarantee of success. As if that was not enough of a paradox, there are many pregnancies that were so easy that people even refer to them as unwanted. Be honest: have you ever caught yourself crying, "But it's not fair!" in a whining childlike voice in any of the following circumstances:

- You seem to be the only couple on Earth bringing up the average conception time. If it were not for you, the average conception time for all of humankind would be just one to three months.

- You have attended weddings while trying to conceive and then, before you know it, find yourself attending a baby shower for this same couple while you continue to chart your ovulation cycle.

- While confiding your plans to friends, they decide this might be a good time to start a family, and you are still *trying* at their baby's christening.

- There seem to be countless images of pregnant media personalities, spanning the ages from sixteen to sixty.

Those are just a few examples of inequities I noticed while our own plans refused to progress. I want to be fully honest even though I am not proud to admit the internal battle that I was fighting in my head. As we were going through this phase, I struggled to be patient and accept that we were having more challenges than we anticipated in our quest to bear a natural child. I vividly remember that even a glimpse of a pregnant woman could bring tears to my eyes. Holidays were especially difficult. Through our nieces and nephews, we were reminded how exciting it would be to hear the pitter patter of little feet that we could call our own running to find Easter eggs or checking to see if Santa had filled their stockings. While we were thrilled to congratulate our friends and family as they one by one announced their wonderful news, I selfishly believed that some of that success was meant for us.

In addition to your Pocket Coach, a support group or structure can really come in handy at these times, because it is really helpful to share with others who have gone through the same situation. Otherwise, some could mistake your grief as a desire for all people to be equally as miserable. Or they may become understandably bored hearing about the ups and more frequent downs of your family-planning progress. Even if you're above concerning yourself with others' reactions, you may question your state of mind without the support of people who fully understand what you're going through emotionally.

Before leaving the topic of infertility, I must reiterate that we were spared a long and difficult path of fertility testing. The option of adoption was presented to us, and that was the avenue we wholeheartedly chose. Having said that, initially I mused whether starting the process would cure our infertility issues. Have you heard about those couples who failed to conceive, decided to adopt, and then miraculously had a natural child? I told myself that if I had to trick my body into thinking that I did not care if it got pregnant, I could do that. Later, I would discover that everything was working out exactly as and when it was supposed to.

People who find out they are not able to have biological children may require counseling before determining whether adoption is suitable for them. Adoption is not a rebound relationship. It is a lifelong commitment that takes another stage of decision-making. Upon learning they are sterile, a couple may undergo a grieving process that must be respected. Only then can they determine if adoption is right for them.

Motivation #2—Tick, tick

There is an increasing number of women whose biological clocks are threatening to detonate if they do not put their reproductive organs to use ASAP. Whether single or in a committed relationship, many childless women who want to bear children become very conscious of each passing birthday. Does this sound familiar? Maybe you are not technically infertile, let alone sterile, but wish to start a family now for your own reasons and are not willing to wait for Mother Nature to co-operate. In case you need me to remind you, the longer you wait, the more difficult it will become.

Not wanting to ignore the male half of the human race, there are men who also want to have a child without delay before they feel they are too well along in years to raise one. They are not racing against a physical fertility clock though, and so they may not totally relate to the female perspective. Women are born with a finite number of eggs and, once they are gone, there is no more production happening in the factory. For the majority of women, menopause is a gradual process that occurs well after they desire to chase a two-year-old around the house on a daily basis. In other cases, early menopause can put a premature stop to child-bearing plans.

With the prevalence of reality TV in this era, I propose a new show. It could be called *My Eggs Are Ripe* and the contestants would all be women seeking to become pregnant. There is a set amount of time allotted to match up the right sperm with the right egg. If you do not win before the commercial break, you go away with a toaster as a consolation prize. Compounding the stress is that you are only given a predetermined number of eggs to play the game, and no two contestants begin with the same number. That doesn't sound fair at all. Luckily for the male contestants, it does not matter how many sperm they use because the producers of the show provide an unlimited supply.

Back to real life. When a girl reaches puberty, every egg her body will ever produce has been created. This is a pretty significant time in her life, and she does not even realize it is happening. Assuming she hits puberty at the average (there we go again) age of eleven, and assuming that a woman is trying to conceive at the age of thirty-six, her eggs are twenty-five years old. Not only has the supply of eggs dwindled, but the lower quality is a factor as well. This will make it harder for a fertilized egg to effectively implant and grow into a fetus.

Although it may seem logical that older women do not release as many eggs as younger women, the opposite is actually true. Women closer to menopause are more likely to release multiple eggs each month. This is the reason that, in the absence of fertility drugs, more twins and multiples are born to older mothers. Conception is as likely to occur (on average) for a more mature woman, but the fertilized egg is more likely to miscarry due to the age of the egg. This often happens before the woman even knows that she is carrying a fertilized egg.

For reasons such as these, an increasing number of single people are adopting children. In particular, the single woman may feel that bearing children naturally is dependent on too many unlikely factors, such as meeting her soulmate before it is too late. Adoption can remove all of that unnecessary pressure while also meeting her maternal needs. More and more international and local adoption regimes are accommodating single parents, and I recognize there may be trepidation among some applicants that they may struggle to fulfill all of their child's needs. If we could possibly survey each of the children in the world who just desperately needs someone to love them, I doubt they would resent having one parent to completely dote on them.

Personally, I found that one of the best perks about being married prior to adopting was that I picked up some extra training to prepare me for raising our children. I will now share some of the lessons I learned through marriage that conditioned me for parenthood as part of our next coaching topic.

One striking similarity between marriage and adoption is that you choose to welcome someone not related to you by blood into your immediate family. No other relationships are likely to bring more joy and fulfillment than these—nor are they likely to introduce as much heartache and disappointment at times. You may experience the odd scary moment when you suddenly realize your life would have been a whole lot simpler without the said child/husband in your life. Fortunately, there are countless more precious moments when you realize how brilliant you are to have made such excellent choices.

On a more practical level, I quickly learned that you simply don't get sick anymore. Well, you do, but not really. Early in our marriage, I discovered what many wives before me have experienced. We may have a fever of 103 degrees Fahrenheit, combined with a violent stomach flu and a touch of strep throat thrown in for good measure, but this minor setback is in no way a match for the common cold our fragile mates may be enduring. Wives learn to silently suffer through illness, realizing that the only person that may have any sympathy for them is their own mother.

This was a valuable lesson for me the first time I was sick as a mother. To stop for the mere flu was a luxury I could not afford. Children still need to be nurtured and dinner still needs to be made. The first time I prepared food for my own loved ones while fighting back the urge to vomit, I knew I had forever crossed the line from dependent to nurturer.

Another valuable lesson that wives or partners can leverage in their role as mother is the ability to build up a tender ego. Through both of these roles, I learned quickly how to praise positive behaviour and reward successful results. If I did need to pass on a suggestion for improvement, it was important to do so in such a way as to not invoke crying, sulking, or violent reactions. It is interesting that the same man who can accept a colleague trashing his work may balk at his wife gently showing him how to properly clean out the sink after shaving. Instead of waiting for her husband to learn to accept these helpful hints, an astute partner will learn how to offer such suggestions in such a way that is not offensive.

One advantage the single adoptive parent enjoys is the absence of jealousy. As far as my own story played out, no matter how deeply I was devoted to my husband, once those maternal instincts kicked in, I was often compelled to pay more attention to the smallest members of the family. This did not always go over well with the biggest member of the family. Although Dave was a pretty independent guy, there was liable to be some jealousy when these cute little beings acquired a large portion of Mama's time and energy.

Motivation #3—Humanitarian reasons

Some of our cheerleaders responded to the news of our two adoptions with overwhelming platitudes about how wonderful Dave and I were for undertaking such a process. To this day, I refute this response. Here we were, desperately wanting children, and we finally had found a beautiful way to realize our dreams.

Sometimes, I felt apologetic for potentially gaining from others' misfortunes, and yet people treated us with a form of reverence, which I sometimes found disconcerting. We were not trying to save the world; we just wanted children!

Ignoring the fact for a moment that adoption fills a void for the adoptive parent(s), the reality is that it may be a turning point for a child who would otherwise have a bleak future. For some adoptive parents, this really was their primary motivating factor, and these are the people who deserve the praise that was bestowed upon us. Sometimes, these angels come in the form of parents who already have children and want to provide an orphan or abandoned child a chance at a fulfilling life instead of conceiving another of their own. Others choose not to have any of their own when there are already so many children in need throughout the world.

Many of the children available for both local and international adoptions have been diagnosed with a medical condition. This does not deter this group of adoptive parents. We met numerous adoptive parents who purposely sought children with special needs because they felt called to help a vulnerable soul with no bright future ahead. Incidentally, many children who are considered special needs in other countries are simply classified as routine medical cases in developed countries. We met children who were available for adoption for conditions such as crossed eyes and displaced hip joints. Sometimes, such a treatable condition can be the factor that precipitates the adoption.

This was the case with our first adoption, as Katja was born with a severe case of bilateral cleft lip and palate. In our corner of the world, this condition is treated from birth with a series of plastic surgeries, orthodontic work, and speech therapy. However, for a baby born in a country that lacks widespread medical coverage, a cleft palate could mean a life sentence, as parents would not be equipped to care for their baby. Without the health-care resources to teach them basics such as feeding their baby and providing the proper tools to do so, parents may be forced to place the baby into the pool of children available for international adoptions. In turn, this very health condition is often the distinguishing factor that allows the child to be adopted out of the country. Sometimes adoptive parents do not face challenges due to negative medical reports. On the contrary, there may be no reports at all. In these cases, it may not be possible to provide adoptive parents with an accurate birthdate, let alone a medical history.

This leads us to an important factor faced by adoptive parents in the decision-making process, particularly if they are seeking an international placement. Often, a congenital disorder is not detectable until the child is born. In most of these cases, natural parents instinctively accept the child's condition as they have already physically and emotionally bonded with the baby. This acceptance may be immediate, or it may take a period of adjustment. The parents' love for their child is not diminished but if given the choice, they would not request that their child be born with a debilitating condition.

Now let's contrast this to the decision-making process in an adoption. At some point, prospective adoptive parents are required to complete a form indicating the diseases, defects, and conditions they will accept in an adopted child. Seeing this question so bluntly worded on the form can be a bit of a reality check, since to this point most people assume there is a perfect, healthy infant waiting for them somewhere in the world.

If you experience this personally, you may initially feel guilty about your urge to check the "none of the above" box. Keep in mind, though, that many people would hesitate to volunteer to become a caregiver of a child with special needs as it may seem like a daunting undertaking. Furthermore, you are asked to make this decision about a theoretical child with whom you have not yet physically connected. The order to these events is reversed in an adoption, as the decision is made to accept a faceless, nameless child's medical condition before a bond has formed.

In addition to selecting the medical condition of an adopted child, the prospective parents may also be asked to select the age. There is no doubt that birthing your own child results in a newborn baby as the end product. With local adoptions, it may be possible to take a baby to its adoptive home directly from the hospital, as we did with our twins' adoption. In the case of international adoptions, most children have passed at least one birthday by the time they are brought into their adoptive homes. Due to stricter laws and more complex procedures, some countries which used to provide relatively quick adoptions now adopt children out at an average age of eighteen months. In other countries, as was the case in Ukraine, the children must be open for adoption within their own country for a period of one year before they are even available for international adoption. Since the paperwork can only start after that point, a child may be two or more years old before landing in their new country.

When we first learned about Katja, she was already three years old. We knew that if we initiated proceedings to adopt her, she would be close to four by the time we brought her home. Many well-intentioned sources warned about the ramifications of adopting an older child, which forced us to evaluate our ability to handle complications that could arise. While I have the utmost sympathy for parents who experience attachment-related challenges that stem from an adoption of an older child, I am happy to report that this was not our experience. Within a matter of weeks, Katja was as attached to us as if she had been with us since birth.

Motivation #4—Pregnancy? No thanks.

There are so many advantages to being pregnant. You can eat as much as you want, strangers smile at you with reverence, and you have an excuse to buy a new wardrobe without a single twinge of guilt. As if that were not enough, you also have a ready-made, universally accepted excuse for bouts of forgetfulness, fatigue, and just plain grouchiness. As enticing as this sounds, you may not think these are good enough reasons to take the plunge and get pregnant.

Perhaps it is the threat of stretch marks and varicose veins that turns you off. Perhaps it is the fear that the epidural will be outlawed one week before your due date. Whatever the reason, your feelings cannot be discounted, and you need not apologize to anybody if you decide pregnancy is not something you wish to experience.

Before reaching such a conclusion, there are several issues you may consider reconciling first. One is that you will never have your own pregnancy and childbirth story. After witnessing our twins' birth as the birth coach, I was quite relieved to have experienced the entire event by observation rather than active participation. Still, when we sent Dave off for some permanent birth control, I remarked that I would miss out on what I had been conditioned to think was a natural occurrence for women to experience. It was not natural in my life and now it never would be.

You also miss out on the opportunity to announce your pregnancy and host your own gender reveal party. On the contrary, the gradual process leading to the decision to adopt makes pinpointing an exact moment to start sharing the news with loved ones more difficult. Once you have decided to allow others to share in your excitement, you may find that they struggle to see your hypothetical child as a physical reality. After all, there is neither an extended tummy to pat nor ultrasound photos to share. The beginning of life is a miracle that invites celebration. The commencement of an adoption launches an administrative network of procedures that invokes stress and uncertainty. This could be one reason why the reactions to both situations are very different. In my own experience, people reacted more enthusiastically upfront when we announced our pregnancy than our adoption plans, which I will explain further in Chapter Four.

For the thirteen weeks I was pregnant, nobody could have possibly known unless I blurted it out, which I was known to do on occasion. After miscarrying, it was a slight consolation that the brief time I was pregnant was not a comfortable experience. Some have insisted that I had just endured the worst part and from that point onward the pregnancy would become easier. I do not believe them, though. Reassurances like these are part of a global conspiracy to convince women into pregnancy so that the human race will continue.

We have all heard tales of women who did not have one second of nausea throughout their pregnancies. Do not ever for a moment assume that you will be one of them. Instead, you may feel continuously ill, tired, and emotional. Women who endure pregnancy must be congratulated and appreciated. Meanwhile, women who actively choose a different path must not feel less a woman because they are not physically contributing to the perpetuation of humanity.

Some people have turned to adoption after experiencing both the thrill of pregnancy and the subsequent crushing blow of one or more miscarriages. Ultimately, they decide they do not want to subject themselves to that potential outcome again. We met a couple who had adopted two precious children after experiencing three heartbreaking miscarriages. This couple chose not to risk a fourth miscarriage and now they have a beautiful family. After having experienced it myself just once, I could envision coming to the same conclusion if I had to endure three miscarriages with no promise for a different outcome the next time.

Pregnancy is not easy on a woman's body. Due to the miraculous work of our Creator, the female body is made to endure the strain of pregnancy, but a medical condition may emerge that, combined with a pregnancy, could create problems for the mother and/or the child. One adoptive mother I met had been diagnosed with severe diabetes, which led her doctor to strongly urge her not to get pregnant. Since she and her husband desperately wanted children, the couple turned to adoption to realize their family goals.

It doesn't matter why

Despite devoting all this time on a few of the more common paths that lead to adoptions, it seems a little late to say that it does not matter why you are adopting—other than to help keep your eye on the goal. That is the truth, though. There could be more than one reason why you have chosen to adopt to expand your family and your motivations may evolve throughout the process. The decision process is unique to each parent, and even to each individual within an adoptive couple. What does matter is that you have decided that your life would be enriched with a child.

At the risk of sounding trite, I will call this a win-win situation, as both parties have much to gain. Congratulations! You have now overcome the first big obstacle. I wish I could say that the whole process is downhill from here. I cannot though, for fear of misrepresentation. Adoption requires patience and a little stubbornness doesn't hurt.

Chapter Three

Baby Steps—Starting the Adoption Paperwork

For whatever reason that is unique to your personal situation, you have decided to adopt a child. Now what? There are many experienced professionals who would take a personal and professional interest in helping you with your goals. Your life will be considerably easier in the coming months if you are able to entrust your adoption into the hands of a reputable adoption agency.

As we had to complete our adoptions on our own, the best suggestion I can offer is to seek a personal recommendation from another adoptive parent when selecting an agency. Otherwise, you may discover that an initial advertised fee can prove to be a significant understatement by the end of the procedure. Once you are already well into the process, you are not going to let a few thousand dollars keep you from your goal, so you will likely proceed regardless of the unanticipated additional expense.

We were not able to use an agency for either of our adoptions due to extenuating circumstances. When adopting the twins, we had to be extremely careful not to let anyone in on our plan for reasons described later in the book. As mentioned previously, when we set out to adopt Katja, there were no adoption agencies in Quebec who were working with Ukraine. Since we had already chosen to adopt from this country due to the connections we made in Switzerland, it was momentarily disheartening when we were told we would not be able to adopt a child from our country of choice.

This was one of the many times throughout our family-building process when we were told our plan would not work. And this was also one example when we proved the naysayers wrong. With no agency to turn to, we simply completed the adoption process ourselves. Well, *simply* is a poor word choice, as it was quite literally a half-time job for the better part of a year. I contemplated adding "project manager for an international adoption" to my curriculum vitae as this project overshadowed any I'd previously considered significant in my professional career.

The first step in the adoption process is to obtain a current and accurate list of all documents required. In the case of an international adoption, this step is complicated by the fact that one must adhere to the requirements of both the local and foreign governments involved. This does not sound difficult in a country where procedures and documentation are common; however, countries that have recently opened their borders to international adoptions often have evolving requirements. In our case, no convenient adoption document checklist existed. We had to forge our own path.

On this topic, we were amazed at the reliance on paper trails in the less computerized countries, including the fact that each document that was prepared for us had to be legalized and stamped so many times we could barely see the original wording underneath. When we eventually visited the Ukrainian bureaucratic offices, we saw computers that were so old compared to what we were accustomed to that I did not even recognize what they were at first. I am not sure when they actually turned on the computers, because most letters were written out long-hand as part of the overall manual process.

The journey may start out as a paper chase that comes with a strict set of rules, but the rules are not communicated at the outset and they can change without warning. To use a cliché, at times it felt like nailing Jell-O to a wall. In some of my more despondent moments throughout the process, I wondered if the Ukrainian officials were personally seeing to it that our experience be especially trying. I found out later that their system was purposely designed to be very stringent about who would be allowed to adopt one of their children.

In fact, international adoptions were halted in Ukraine for a full year to give the officials the time and opportunity to establish a fair adoption system. Prior to this one-year moratorium, the adoption industry had become very corrupt and harmful to some of the children involved. Among the worst of the horror stories we heard involved adopted children being sold for body parts. Considering the atrocity of stories like this, it was understandable that the Ukrainian officials made it a priority to ensure their children were given a better life. And if that meant we needed to obtain some extra documents and more rubber stamps to satisfy the rules, the safety of the children was worth the inconvenience.

In order to forge a relationship with the Ukrainian government, we had to prove that we were decent, law-abiding citizens. It would have been much easier for us if they could have merely telephoned our mothers for a reference. Instead, they needed an extensive dossier of letters and reports written by everyone from doctors to the bank to the police. If you have gone through the process, perhaps you remarked afterward how much better you knew yourself when it was done. At the end of this stage, you will have obtained and supplied diverse pieces of personal information, including the state of your physical and financial health and detailed data about your family members.

I haven't forgotten my vision for this book. I vowed I would not merely recite lists of legal requirements to complete an adoption. In keeping with that promise, I will not delve into the depths of detail regarding all of the information we supplied, to whom, and when. Besides, it would not be relevant for anyone else since the requirements are not only changing but are also a function of the adoptive parents' place of residence, as well as that of the adopted child. However, there is one document that deserves an honourary mention. It is common to all adoptions, whether local or international, and is the most time-consuming (and expensive) document to obtain. Any adoptive parent would likely agree that the granddaddy of all documents is the home study.

The Home Study

If you are not familiar with this term, prepare to become so if you plan to adopt. Indeed, prepare to make it one of the most important phrases in your daily vocabulary. The home study represents a very thorough process whereby a social worker is assigned to interview you (and your partner, if applicable) several times, including once in your home, culminating in a written report that outlines your past and present lives. The idea is to ultimately determine whether you have the means to care for a child on multiple bases, including financial, psychological, and emotional. Throughout the process, you may question the relevance of some of the material.

At all times, it is important to be on friendly terms with the social worker. No matter your personal view of the home study formalities, try to show nothing but joy for the opportunity to pay someone a lot of money to document your life history. You may find that your idea of speeding up the process is at the opposite end of the spectrum to that of the social worker. Even if both parties are committed to hasten the outcome, the process will still take a minimum of three to four months.

This is the step that not only lies on the critical path, but basic-ally *is* the critical path. Nothing can start until the home study is completed. Since that requires several scheduled interviews and waiting for an overworked social worker to finish your report, you may become frustrated at the lack of control over the timing of the situation. Do not show your stress and irritation or you may have to endure and pay for an extra session on how to handle your stress as a parent!

For our first adoption, time was of the essence. When we set out to adopt Katja, we knew that she was aged three years and two months and that, with every month that passed, she was missing critical bonding and stimulation opportunities. Her birthday is the thirteenth of June, and I remember that on the thirteenth of each month I was acutely aware that we had lost another month of her life. In most jurisdictions, a home study must be completed within one year of the adoption. Since our adoptions were four-teen months apart, we had the unique privilege of undergoing the home study process twice within a short period of time. In the case of the twins' adoption, we tried to prepare as much of the paperwork as possible before they were born. This was not straightforward for reasons I will divulge later.

I was encouraged when the social worker performing our first home study stated that our situation would be relatively easy to document, which I thought at first was her kind way of saying that our lives were boring! I also naively assumed that meant the home study would be a miraculously short and inexpensive process for us. And yet, it required five sets of interviews, twice the fees that we expected, and approximately three more months to complete than we anticipated.

Now that I can look back a little more objectively, and due to the passage of several years since being subjected to the process, I can see that it was valuable for us. It provided an opportunity to slow down and catch our breath in a very emotional time. The greatest nugget of wisdom we received came from the social worker who performed our first home study. Dave and I were discussing our plans for our adopted child and how we would ensure she could go to university. The social worker reminded us that no parent—natural or adoptive—can be sure of a child's future. She knew that we would be adopting a child who spent her first four years in an orphanage, so automatically there could be implications affecting her education path. We were reminded that parenthood requires loving our children for who they are, and not some preconceived notion about who we think they should be and what they must become.

Within the entire international adoption project, the home study and subsequent translation constituted approximately one-quarter of the total expenses including travel. In the case of our local adoption, the home study comprised the majority of all costs involved. Any expense is relative and so if you compare the home study to a home purchase, the home study is clearly not significant. On the other hand, if you compare it to a single mortgage payment, it becomes much more important.

Paying this money was even more frustrating when I realized that I could have written most of the report myself. The report was primarily an objective description of our backgrounds and current situation. We provided factual information about our parents, siblings and childhoods. Then we were required to discuss how Dave and I met and came to marry. We were asked about our careers, hobbies, and interests. Whenever a question was repeated from an earlier session, I envisioned stacks of money flying out the social worker's window. Once our children were with us, these images quickly faded in the same way I imagine a natural mother's memory of labour pains wane over time.

By the time our first home study was completed, the majority of the other fourteen documents I had traipsed around Montreal to gather were already translated, which is a requirement for many international adoptions. As an aside, our translator conveniently managed to double his fees from the time of our first to last translations. We counted ourselves lucky as he hinted that he might triple them. I think he saw dollar signs above my head every time I walked into his small, quaint office. In all fairness, he tried to help us when he warned us to ask our social worker to make the home study as short as possible. Thinking this sounded like a brilliant suggestion, I passed it on at our next session only to be informed that the report had to be written in compliance with strict international conventions. The standard length of such a report was typically eight to ten pages. Do not ask me why, then, our simple case resulted in a report of fourteen pages.

My intent is not to depict a gloomy picture designed to turn you completely against the home study. I am merely being honest about our experiences because I wish someone had enlightened me at the beginning of our process to set our expectations appropriately. Indulging in self-analysis can be entertaining, even if you have to pay your audience. However, as humans, we often feel stress when circumstances do not meet our expectations. Had I expected the home study to consume as much time and resources as it did, the process would not have been so frustrating. When we were undergoing our second home study, I was much more prepared for a lengthy and costly process. This time, we were pleasantly surprised as the completion time and price tag attached were both significantly reduced, and of course no translations were required.

Early on in our first home study journey, the social worker warned us that, at the end of it all, we would either want to postpone the adoption or would be more committed than ever. We experienced the latter. Our commitment was strengthened through these open discussions and became key during some of the most challenging times that we experienced in the months ahead.

At one point, I remarked on how unfortunate it was that biological parents do not typically have the opportunity to experience pre-parental counselling. The whole process reminded me of our marriage preparation courses. Before earning the right to be married, we were required to participate in discussions with our minister about any potential issues with which we might be faced throughout our marriage. It is much more effective to do so before the marriage certificate is signed. In much the same way, overall it was a valuable exercise for us to reflect on how we would raise our children before we were in the throes of parenthood.

Chapter Four

Reactions of Others & How to Prepare for Them

Our two adoptions were different in every possible way. With Katja, we experienced an international adoption of a toddler and had little knowledge of the birth parents or of the life she experienced in the orphanage. Subsequently, we experienced a local adoption of twin infants who we carried home from the hospital. Due to the diversity of the two stories, I will tell them separately in later chapters.

There was one common experience in both situations. At some point, we announced our intentions to adopt publicly, and the reactions were mixed. I must mention upfront, and then strongly reinforce throughout our story, that any trepidation expressed by those in our inner circle was motivated by a genuine concern that we would suffer heartbreak due to an unsuccessful result. As it turned out, that risk became very real at multiple times. All apprehensions instantly vanished as soon as we were in the clear and our children were safely at home with us.

It is not possible to say at what point is the best to tell people about your intentions. During our brief thirteen-week pregnancy, I announced my condition before the recommended three-month stage. Even though this required following up with phone calls after the miscarriage to provide updates, I did not regret sharing the news early on. Similarly, we started telling people of our adoption plans at the stage I equated with being one month pregnant in that we had just started to gather information. As soon as we were committed to our adoptions, we felt strongly that we were on a one-way street with no going back and so chose to be very open about our plans. This may be too early for some if they do not want to risk having to tell people they've changed their course of action down the road or that it did not work out. If I was coaching you, we could work through different scenarios to the end to determine how you want to manage your communication strategy. To help you prepare, I have an observation to share.

I found that people reacted very differently to the news of my pregnancy than to the news of both of our adoption plans. In many cases, people just do not know what to say as they lack personal experience from which to draw. It will not seem real to them because there is no physical evidence to observe, unless of course you want to pass around your home study report. Since we all have an idea what reaction to expect when we announce a pregnancy, I would now like to focus on what you may expect when you send out your We are Adopting announcements.

Reaction 1: Immediate Acceptance and Support

The angels in your midst who exhibit this reaction were purposely placed there. You need them. There will be some in your cheering section who initially may greet your news with one of the other responses I will describe in the following sections. Do not give up on them as they may also turn out to be your greatest sources of support. In our case, we would have never been able to bring Katja home when we did without the active support of our close family and friends.

In the early stages, at times I was overwhelmed by the extent to which perfect strangers rejoiced in our news. For example, my sister-in-law's colleague was emotionally involved in our proceedings from the very beginning. It didn't matter that we had never met this woman and probably never would since we lived on opposite ends of the country. She rejoiced and wept with us as she willingly chose to follow our emotional journey. When we finally brought Katja home, this lovely stranger pleaded to see photos and even mailed a welcome home gift for her.

I would meet other random strangers along my travels who instantly became champions of our cause. Part of the preparation for our first trip to Ukraine was to load up on gifts for government workers and officials who were directly involved in our adoption. I felt conspicuous as I made my way to the cashier with a heaping cart of chocolates and other gift items. Not surprisingly, the store employees and other shoppers commented on my excessive sweet tooth. I told them who the chocolates were for and instantly my story captured the attention of everyone in earshot. My newfound friends wanted to hear all adoption details. They were captivated by our story, and some offered heartwarming stories about others they knew who had travelled a similar path. This was one of multiple times that complete strangers cheered us on.

These incidents were often a much-needed respite from the grind of administrative adoption details and setbacks encountered. Much like refreshment spots along the course of a marathon, these touchpoints recharged my batteries just enough to make it to the next stage. While the support of close friends and family is more meaningful than that offered by strangers in the candy section of a department store, some days it was the endorsement of outsiders that helped me through a given day. There were several times when the outcome of our adoptions looked bleak, and it felt tempting to give up for a fleeting moment. Meeting immediate supporters who were not vested in our lives, and therefore not worried about our potential suffering, allowed me to feed off their energy and optimism at times when my own was waning.

Before alienating our inner circle by insinuating they were not supportive of our plans, let me be clear that this could not be further from the truth. Along with expressing concern for our emotional well-being, our loved ones were very excited and happy for us at the same time. I distinctly recall returning home after one particularly frustrating day of dealing with red tape in Katja's adoption. Such events blurred together and so I can't recall exactly what happened. What I do recall is coming home to discover a large parcel had been delivered to our door. Inside were piles of clothes and accessories for a little girl sent by a close family member.

The contents contrasted sharply with the adoption-related red tape that had dominated my attention throughout that particular day. Suddenly, I was like a little child at Christmas. I neatly arranged the clothes in the living room and imagined them floating around the room, powered by our daughter's body and limbs. I needed that physical reminder of the true goal. Contrary to the way I felt earlier that day, we were *not* on a mission to gather a dossier of legal documents. We were on an exciting journey to bring Katja into our lives and the documents were merely the means to that end. I received all the encouragement I needed to get through what lay ahead the next day thanks to the support of our loving family back home.

Reaction 2: Accolades: You are Great and Courageous

This reaction still perplexes me. Here we were being blessed with precious children—and without the pains of childbirth, I might add. For some reason, people congratulated us for making some kind of sacrifice. At first, I was intimidated by this reaction, as we did not intend to commit some brave and generous act. We just wanted to build our family.

Many people will think you are brave because they cannot see themselves entering the lesser travelled adoption territory and so project their reservations onto your situation. Do not bother correcting people who react to you in this way. Second only to *Reaction 1* of immediate acceptance and support, this is the easiest reaction to manage.

Reaction 3: Everyone has a Horror Story

We have all observed peoples' reactions when a pregnant woman announces her news to a group of friends, family, colleagues, or even mere acquaintances. She is typically greeted with smiles, congratulations, and overall excitement. Sometimes the overzealousness of the well-wishers causes them to share stories of their own forty-eight-hour death-defying labour-and-delivery saga—but overall, the reaction is very positive. For example, you do not typically hear: "Do you realize it's possible you will miscarry or experience other terrible complications?". When we announced our pregnancy within the first trimester, nobody ever cautioned me (to my face) that I might miscarry. At best, that reaction would be considered rude and, at worst, heartless.

In this way, the adoption experience was very different for us from the natural family expansion experience. When we announced our intentions to adopt, some felt compelled to warn us about two different types of horror stories.

Story type number one was of adoptions that were close to fruition, only to be thwarted by a birth mother who changed her mind at the final hour. As you will learn, our twins' adoption was unique in that we could not start any formal proceedings until after they were born. As a result, we had no legal recourse if their birth mother changed her mind, even months after they were born. Nobody needed to remind us of this risk. Still, some people we encountered were concerned we could end up severely disappointed and so wanted to be sure we were well-informed about this possibility.

Story type number two dealt with various scenarios in which the adopted child was unable to adapt, assimilate, or attach to their new parents. Our adoption of Katja was fodder for such stories. She was almost four years old, had some known medical issues, was improperly diagnosed with others, and was from a faraway land and so would not understand a word we said for some time. There was so much potential for her entry into her new life to go off the rails. I am delighted to report that our experience with Katja in those first weeks and months went more smoothly than we could have dared to hope. If we had taken the tales too seriously, perhaps we would have second-guessed our plans and never found out. While we gleaned some insights from the stories shared with us, we did not let others' adverse experiences deter us from our own family expansion plan.

If the majority of adoption stories you hear are disheartening, you are not hearing a representative sample. As I became more entrenched in the world of adoption, I heard many beautiful success stories. My belief is that the vast majority of adoption cases are successful, for both the child and the family. Admittedly, there is no guarantee of smooth sailing, but this is perfectly normal in the messy and unpredictable world of parenthood.

The important point to remember is that no child—adopted or otherwise—comes with a money-back guarantee. Parenting takes a commitment, something that's helpful to keep in mind when you encounter negative stories in the initial stages. To offer up one more analogy, we all hear statistics about the divorce rate, and yet marriages continue to occur. We typically don't warn an engaged couple about what could go wrong in their marriage. No, we offer them hope. If you are not hearing such words of hope during your adoption journey, it is important to stay focused on your goal and visualize the wonderful things in store for you and your family. Hopefully our story can help reassure you that adoption can work for you too.

Reaction 4: Apprehension

I briefly referred to a reaction of concern as a contrast to the immediate support often received by strangers. As this response is most likely to be exhibited by those closest to you, I will share a little more about our own story in case it helps you to navigate your own personal situation.

Dave and I are very lucky in that we both come from supportive and loving families. Therefore, we were a bit surprised at the outset when some people close to us reacted with apprehension, until I learned that this is a very common response. In this case, the horror stories outlined in the previous section are not overtly discussed. Instead, loved ones may exhibit a reaction that appears to be a mixture of fear and detachment. This is only fair, since they, too, have heard the adoption horror stories. Before judging your concerned inner circle too harshly, remember that you likely spent weeks, months, or even years concluding that adoption was the right option for you. You must allow your family their own time to believe your dreams could be fulfilled.

In order to combat this reaction, I found that it helped to keep everyone abreast of our progress in real time. At first, there may not be a lot of feedback, but eventually the guards come down and, one by one, they became emotionally invested as well. It does help if you are able to have some physical evidence of the child, such as pictures and information files. I encourage you to share those with the people in your inner circle with whom you discuss your plans. Also, you may need to continually remind yourself about the critical point I have reinforced multiple times. Those who initially exhibit apprehension about your plans to adopt often become part of your most enthusiastic support group.

For example, my parents are as devoted to their grandchildren as anyone could be, and so I wondered why they were hesitant to inquire about our adoption progress at first. Instinctively I knew that their lack of reaction was deliberate. They did not want me to attach emotionally to potential children who may never materialize. I vividly recall discussing this with my mother before we went to Ukraine the first time. Her explanation was the one I'd predicted. She confirmed that they were captivated and thrilled about the prospect of our adoption plans. They could not wait to meet their new grandchild, should it work out in our favour. They were just worried that we would be disappointed if it did not, and so tried not to feed the excitement.

Once I learned not to misconstrue apprehension for disapproval, I came to appreciate this reaction as it was a sign of love and concern for us. By the time Katja came home, my parents did not hesitate to travel across the country to meet her and they instantly attached to each other. Katja was their grandchild as much as if she had known them her whole life. Both sides fell in love instantly and any initial fears about potential heartbreak for us became a distant memory.

Reaction 5: Are You Ready for This?

Is anyone ever ready to have their first child? Before you actually have a child in your home who is completely dependent upon you, do you really know what that means? The longer we wait, I believe, the more difficult it becomes to uproot our lives for the little bundle that will soon rule our world. Even if someone had attempted to paint a picture of what our lives would be like after children, I do not think I would have fully grasped what that meant until after the fact. I would have underestimated how sleep deprived I would become. I would not have realized that losing all personal time and space was an adjustment. At the same time, I would not have understood how instantly I could become attached to a little being to the point where I could not imagine life without them.

From my observations and experience, both adoptive and natural parents often end up on the receiving end of advice about how their lives are about to be dramatically altered, but there are differences in the overall delivery of the message. In general, people want to be supportive and excited for the parents-to-be. If they view adoption as coming with a back-door policy, the tone may be more of a warning of the ramifications of parenthood than a lighthearted ribbing. This may prevail even to the point when you have your papers in hand and are ready to either board a plane or begin court proceedings.

When you are asked if you are ready to become a parent, I recommend replying honestly that of course you are not. Clearly, you are not setting out to simplify your life if you plan to have a child. Ironically, it is precisely because some people waited so long for the perfect time to be ready that they find themselves on the adoption path in the first place.

On this note, there can be different preparation required for adopting an older child than a newborn. With a new baby, you are handed a brand new unopened can of Play-Doh for you and only you to begin the shaping process. As your baby grows and develops, you will experience the changes gradually, so are less likely to be shocked by unexpected behaviours. In adopting an older child, you take on an unknown personality. I compare this to marriage, but without the luxury of a dating process to get to know the person in advance.

Adopting an older child means you will also have to accept that you cannot know everything that happened in the first few years of your child's life and so may be mopping up the after-effects of neglect, or even abuse. On the positive side, Katja helped us ease into parenthood as she came to us already toilet-trained, able to feed herself, and was accustomed to sleeping through the night. We had bypassed that stage of constant physical dependency that can drain all of the energy of a parent with a newborn baby.

Instead, we had a curious, observant little girl who wanted to see and experience everything around her. She shadowed me around the house like a little sponge, soaking up everything I said and did. For the first time in my life, I was very conscious of every action I made, fearful that a wrong move would warp her mind forever. I found this constant interaction tiring as I felt on display at all times. I tried to explain it to Dave in terms of work so he could relate to my fatigue. I compared my day to him being in his office, trying to work, while people constantly interrupted him with the same questions from morning to night. He got the point.

This brings up another coachable moment. There were two paradoxes I identified as a new mom that I will share in case they help you to prepare for this role:

1. *I was extremely busy but never got anything done*—Outside of my motherhood career, I am a goal-oriented list-maker and always have been. Now, suddenly, there was no point making a list because it would have seemed pretty pathetic. *Feed child, clean up, dress child, provide stimulating activity, prepare food, clean up, repeat.* These little creatures could keep me occupied all day, but at the end of it, I did not feel like I had accomplished anything. When Dave returned home after work, he would inquire what I had done that day. I don't think his intent was malicious. He was likely just curious. I had no response beyond that I had kept the kids alive, and this may have been relayed with a hint of annoyance and a dash of sarcasm. He eventually learned not to ask this question.

2. *At times, I felt isolated and lonely, although I never had a moment to myself.* To the extent possible, the kids and I would set off on field trips and visit mom groups, friends and family. Still, much of our time was spent at home, especially when they were very young. For the most part I reveled in this opportunity, but there were times when I missed the bigger world that existed beyond our property lines. After a challenging day, Dave would generously offer to stay with the children so I could leave and get some time to myself. Again, his intentions were completely

honourable, and once again clueless. The last thing I wanted was to be alone, even if it seemed like I wanted to be left alone. I realize that makes no logical sense.

Before concluding this chapter on people's reactions, I must admit to times in my life when, in retrospect, I wish I could take back my negative reaction to another's unfortunate situation. This type of negativity typically stems from deeper emotions, such as fear or jealousy. Or sometimes it may just be a bad case of foot-in-the-mouthitis.

I recall an incident in Montreal in which I exhibited all of the above. We were nearing the end of our first adoption proceedings and my nerves were raw. I could not blame my fragile state on hormones, but on high and rising stress levels brought on by uncertainty and the constant outflow of money. I thought our situation was the most difficult on Earth and so did not have as much empathy for mothers around me as I might have.

Right around this time a woman from our church gave birth to her second child, after which she suffered five weeks of extreme post-partum depression. Obviously, this is not a state I have ever experienced, and for that I am truly thankful. In my clear and lucid state today, I have deep sympathy for anyone touched by this syndrome and I comprehend that it in no way reflects the love a mother has for her new baby.

Although I understood all of this at the time, I was consumed with our own family-planning efforts. We were not only in the throes of adoption stress, but we had no signs of success on the horizon. The sight of new mothers compounded my frustration as I felt resentful of the blessings bestowed on them, and then subsequently felt guilty for my envy. It was a vicious cycle and not one of my prouder moments. I refuse to use this as an excuse for my reaction to this new mother in pain, as there is no justification for what I was about to say. What I do know is that my lack of support for her was rooted in my own negative feelings and had nothing to do with her situation.

Basically, I blurted out that since a child was my number-one wish in the world, I could not understand how anyone would be depressed after giving and receiving the miracle of life. What a terrible and heartless thing for me to say! But it was too late. The words had escaped my mouth and, before I knew it, our conversation was interrupted, and I was left soaking in the realization that I was the most insensitive and selfish human being at that moment.

I was able to ease my conscience the next week when I profusely apologized for my ignorance. Throughout the week I had tried to downplay the incident as maybe not quite as awful as I remembered. But as it turned out, I had not imagined my lack of diplomacy, as she knew what I was about to address before I even began. I was grateful that she forgave me on the spot. It took me a little longer to forgive myself.

What this incident did for me was highlight that my negative reaction came from my own feelings and that revelation helped me to handle any negative reactions we would experience to our adoption plans. I understood that they were primarily motivated by others' fear that we would become emotionally, if not financially, bankrupt at the end of our journey if we came away empty-handed. Perhaps some feared for their own emotions in case they became attached to a child they would never meet. Once I fully grasped the root cause, it helped me to process the different responses we encountered to our adoption plans.

I hope that my words do not discourage you from sharing your plans with friends and family, whose support you will also require at various times. I just want to help you avoid feelings of disappointment if you do not receive the reaction you anticipate at first. Have faith that your confidantes will be elated to witness this miracle come into your and their lives. Meanwhile, I believe in your plans and will continue to support you by sharing our story. First, we have one more general topic to explore a little deeper.

Chapter Five

Attachment: Will Our Child Like Us? (and vice versa)

W hat if our adopted child does not like us? What if we do not bond with the child? We all know that other people's children are noisy, messy, and smell funny. Perhaps you fear that your adopted child will be like other people's children. This is a normal concern. Adoptive parents do not have the corner on this market, as some biological parents also fear they will not attach to their unborn child.

Dealing with the attachment issue was a very different experience for Dave and myself. This is not terribly surprising considering our diverse reactions in virtually all emotionally charged situations in life. My three-month pregnancy was such an example of the two of us in the same storm but riding in completely different boats. Within hours of learning about my condition, I was already committed to the microscopic-sized human form in my still unexpanded stomach. For Dave, it was a non-event. At first, he repeatedly asked me if I really thought I was pregnant! For him, there was no real child while, for me, the child was as real as my nausea. Therefore, when the miscarriage occurred, I mourned the loss of a child. Dave, meanwhile, expressed a bit of sadness that we almost had a child. The difference is subtle but significant in terms of the emotional impact each turn of events had on us.

Similarly, when we started the adoption process, our hypothetical child was real to me as soon as I completed the initial phone call of inquiry. Dave stayed more reserved and clinical about his parental instincts. His attitude was that he would believe it when he saw some proof that it would become a physical reality. Do not get me wrong. He was very co-operative, even for those killer blood tests, but he remained emotionally distant at this stage. It was not until we reached the much later steps of booking plane tickets that Dave was fully emotionally invested. By the time Katja was a physical reality in our home, Dave was as committed to her as if he had fathered her from conception.

There are two parties that are required to bond together. No matter how certain you are that you will love your adopted child, there are no guarantees that the child will have the ability to return your affections initially. Attachment disorder syndrome is a book in itself and so I will merely touch on a few highlights based on our personal experiences. If such a disorder becomes part of your life, you may find it necessary to seek professional help to conquer it.

We were fortunate in that Katja's first years did not reflect the worst-case-scenario stories we had heard. In some orphanages, the children are neglected to the extreme that the babies develop flat heads and cannot hold their heads up because they have lay in cribs all day. Such neglect can have long-lasting effects the adoptive parent may not feel capable of managing on their own.

There are two different types of attachment disorders. The more common situation involves children who cannot bear to be touched or make direct eye contact. Some of these children cannot even walk barefoot as the sensation of touch on their feet is too traumatic for them. A second stream of attachment disorders is manifested by children who will try to attach to any adult. While this may not sound completely negative, it can become disruptive if the child cannot distinguish between parents and strangers and so does not form a real relationship with anyone. I remember one case in which an adoptive mother was concerned because her child would run up and try to connect with every female he encountered—even the check-out woman at the grocery store was fair game. This child had difficulty understanding that the mother he lived with was his very own nurturer—and that nobody else would spontaneously substitute into that role.

Not all adopted children exhibit any of these symptoms, regardless of the age of adoption. Cases have been documented of children adopted as early as six to eight months who were never able to bond with their parents. Then you have lucky parents such as us. Within a matter of days and weeks, Katja had bonded to us and formed true relationships with multiple family members. In her first months, she made fast friendships with the little girl next door, as well as a couple of girls at the daycare. So, contrary to what was forewarned to us before Katja's adoption, it *is* possible for some children to learn how to bond at an advanced age.

When I think about the bond from the adoptive parents' perspective, it reminds me of the premarital courses in which Dave and I learned about the four different types of love. Each definition's meaning is rooted in a different Latin word for love. The Latin-speaking people of ancient times were smart enough to recognize that love is a multi-faceted beast and that it is possible to have different types of love for different people and so gave each a distinct name. They are as follows:

1. *Phileo—Brotherly love*—It is not surprising that Philadelphia is nicknamed the city of brotherly love. Phileo refers to the affection we feel for friends and family because we value their friendship. We like to spend time together and typically have common interests that bond us together.

2. *Storge—Protective love*—You are playing with a baby bear cub when suddenly the mother appears from nowhere. You are bound to feel a little concerned, in case the mother bear is overcome by the storge she feels for her baby. She instinctually feels a need to protect her offspring from harm. Another example of storge may even be exhibited by an older brother who delights in taunting his younger brother in the confines of their own home. But, when that same brother hears a third party on the school playground taking the same liberties with his flesh and blood, he rushes to his little brother's defense. Although he would never want to admit it aloud, the older brother shows he has storge for his sibling.

3. *Eros—Erotic love*—There is no need to really expand on this topic. If you want further information on eros, please consult the *How to Get Pregnant* section of the bookstore.

4. *Agape—Committed love*—Dave and I learned during our premarital classes that agape is the one factor that can separate a successful marriage from an unsuccessful one. By success, I do not just mean that the marriage does not end with a trip to the lawyer, but that the needs of both parties are met through the marriage. In order to have such a marriage, both partners must actively decide that, no matter

what, they will be committed to their partner. Although this may sound like a death sentence, it does not feel that way if you have agape for your spouse.

There are bound to be times when spouses do not feel particularly friendly toward each other. Even as *phileo* may wane during these stressful periods, the commitment inherent in *agape* includes the promise to work together through these times and become friends again. Also, there are times when one partner does not feel *eros* toward the other. It is *agape* that prevents either of the couple from seeking gratification outside of the marriage unit. In summary, *agape* requires that a decision is made to love your spouse no matter what happens. This will come in handy as you learn intimately every one of their annoying—I mean endearing—habits.

I challenge you to consider loving an adopted child the same way that we were challenged to learn about love within the context of marriage. Even when children—adopted or biological—present us with challenges, the prevailing emotion needs to be the joy these little challenge-makers have brought to our households. If that fails, just remember the commitment of love you made when you adopted your child, and you will get through those moments.

Sadly, there are cases in which *agape* is not present in parent-child relationships and sometimes it is because the parents did not consciously decide they wanted to have a baby. With adoption, a conscious commitment must be made to an unknown child before the papers are signed. Furthermore, throughout the long paperwork trail, there are several opportunities to stop the process. By the time the adoption is completed, the parents have unknowingly built up a large *agape* bank account in the name of their child.

We were not destined to have natural children, but I have met numerous parents who have a family comprised of both natural and adopted children. Each situation is different, but one common thread within every family was that the parents had no distinction in bonding with any of their children. I love the following quote from writer Bob Constantine on this topic: "I have four children. Two are adopted. I forget which two."

From my experience, I can say that I cannot imagine having a deeper bond with any child than I do with our three. Almost as soon as Katja was with us, there was no doubt in her mind who her parents were and what that meant for her. She was not pleased when Mama was not in her sight. I remember the first time I left Katja at the daycare. She had only been with us for four months and we decided it might help promote her language and social skills to interact with other children. We determined that she would attend the daycare three mornings each week, and the first time I dropped her off, she and I both suffered separation anxiety. We both recovered, but it was a difficult experience.

As I gave Katja a tearful hug goodbye, the daycare workers consoled me by remarking what a good sign it was that Katja was very attached to me. They assured me that this was an important step in her (and my) development. They found it hard to believe she had only been with us such a short time, when they saw she responded to us in the same manner as any other child at the daycare did with their parents. In the same way, we formed a strong and instant connection with the twins immediately following their birth.

Speaking of Katja and the twins, now it is finally time to proceed with their adoptions!

PART TWO

Katja – International Adoption of a Toddler

Bureaucracy

International Travel

Immigration Complications

Lobbying to Bring Katja Home

Return to Ukraine

We Meet the Birth Parents

Chapter Six

Let the Bureaucratic Battles Begin

Several years ago, I hired an agent in order to publish this book through the traditional channels. One large and very reputable firm was ready to proceed but with one caveat. They wanted the book to cater to an audience interested in adopting by providing step-by-step guidance along the way. They wanted the end product to contain lists of processes and procedures that one could follow in order to complete an adoption successfully. I have no doubt that such a book would be of value to many. The only problem was that I could not write it.

As you will soon discover, our adoptions were unorthodox, to say the least. It is doubtful that the details in our approach would be relevant to the masses. I am still going to share some of them for a different reason. I am hoping our experiences will not only help some realize their adoption dreams, but also any goal in life where the stakes really matter.

The lesson I will reinforce in this section is the importance of creating a compelling vision and hanging, sometimes clinging, onto it when you encounter obstacles. Tangible representations of that vision can be instrumental in keeping it front and centre. For me, one was in the form of a broken dresser knob, which I will fully explain a little later. As well, we had pictures of Katja tacked onto our fridge that Vic Jackopson sent at the very beginning of our journey. On the most trying of days, I would stand and stare at those photographs in the hopes that Katja would spring from them and come alive in the kitchen. When that didn't happen, I knew I had to get up the next morning and conquer whatever battles presented themselves.

I will be successful in writing this section if you find it a little frustrating to read. This is not because I derive pleasure from others' misery. Quite the opposite! My goal is to underline the role our vision played by giving you a sense of what we experienced during the months leading up to Katja's adoption, particularly when it felt like we were getting nowhere. It would have been so easy to give up without a clear line of sight to our vision. This is an example I use in leadership training to this day, as it is applicable to all walks of life.

As mentioned previously, we did not have the luxury of using an adoption agency if we chose to proceed with the specific situations presented to us, and you can avoid a significant amount of the frustration we encountered if you are able to hire a reputable adoption agency. Although this means paying others to do your legwork, by reading about our struggles you may suddenly feel that your adoption agency's fees do not seem so exorbitant after all.

In the beginning stages, an adoption journey resembles one big paper chase. Although the previously discussed home study document was only one of more than a dozen that we had to collect over a span of six months, it stands out from the others as second to none in terms of the investment of time, effort, and money it took to compile. Each of the other documents contributed its fair share of logistical challenges and so they collectively deserve an honourable mention. They included bank records, medical reports, reference letters, proof of employment, police reports and various vital statistics records to name a few.

Understandably, many overseas adoptions require that every word on every page of each precious and lengthy document be translated into the official language of the adopted child's birth country before receiving an official rubber stamp. By official, I mean the kind you have to pay to receive. In retrospect, I wish we had found two or three certified translators in the Montreal area. Unfortunately, I was challenged to find even one qualified Ukrainian translator who also owned one of those special rubber stamps. I learned that we were especially vulnerable because our documents had to be translated into a language not commonly spoken by locals. It seemed to me that each trip to our Ukrainian translator in Montreal was more expensive than the last when he realized that he was on the winning side of the supply and demand curve. A backup translator could potentially hedge against rising costs within a fee structure that was anything but structured. Perhaps I was just confused, I mused, as I admired our translator's brand-new Mercedes on my last visit to his run-down office.

After your translated documents are christened with their first rubber stamp by a certified translator, they are ready for the even bigger and more expensive official rubber stamp from the embassy. This step is referred to as *legalizing* your documents. It was critical that our translator's rubber stamp be acceptable to the Ukrainian embassy or else our documents could not be legalized.

Despite my whining, it was reasonable that the Ukrainian

officials required proof that the documents we submitted were legitimate. The role of the Ukrainian embassy in Canada was to certify both the authenticity of the document and the accuracy of the translation. That way, when the documents were received by the officials in Ukraine, they could be assured that they contained accurate information from a credible source and so these rubber stamps were more than symbolic. Legalizing our documents was on the critical path of our adoption project and had to be bought at any price. There was no discount Ukrainian embassy from which I could barter a lower price and so once again I was a buyer in a seller's market.

Once our documents were completed, translated, and legalized, it was time to set them free. I imagined how terrifying it must be for parents to send a child away to college. I have now experienced this firsthand, but at the time I wondered whether our release of documents to this faraway land was somewhat comparable. For the last several months, we had laboured over these precious papers, while trying to keep pace with the associated and escalating expenses.

The package we eventually released, along with our best wishes, contained a high degree of emotional and financial investment. This thought did not escape me as I handed the life-altering documents to the courier. Realizing the loss of these documents would result in another several months of bureaucratic battles, I wrapped the package with an extra layer of prayers to help carry it successfully through the postal system. I was less apprehensive about its journey from Montreal to Austria than I was from that point forward. Although the second leg of the trip was much shorter, I believe my trepidation was caused by fear of the unknown, as the package would be entering territory that, at that point, I had never personally visited. I could not visualize any component of the Ukrainian postal system and this was unnerving for me.

Mercifully for my nervous and digestive system, our documents were escorted by a modern tracing system. I could (and did) phone the local courier every day to find out their whereabouts. By Day 3, they had already journeyed from Montreal to Warsaw, Poland. They were due to arrive in Kiev by the end of Day 4. With naivety and hope, I phoned the courier at the end of Day 4 to discover that our package was delinquent in reaching its destination. I envisioned it sitting in some backroom office. I was sure nobody would even remember it was there. Somebody might have mistaken it for some plain, regular package. It was at this point I had to let faith take over. We were not in control and had done all we could; all that was left was to wait. And when that was not enough, I could always try calling the courier one more time to see if there was an update.

We later discovered that the documents had been delayed on Day 4 because they had missed their flight connection. Did they not understand their significance? Did they decide to discover downtown Warsaw and then misjudge the amount of time to get back to the airport? I was quite disappointed, as I thought I had given them ample warnings to stick to the travel schedule.

By Day 5, my courier Mike and I were great friends. He took a special interest in tracing our package's location and graciously kept me informed. Mike was always patient when answering my numerous phone calls to check up on the progress, or lack thereof, of our precious-yet-tardy package. On Day 9, he was able to call me with the highly-anticipated news that the documents had finally reached their intended destination—the adoption centre in Kiev. I no longer cared that we had paid a lot of money to courier a package that took nine full days to be delivered. The package was safe and in the hands of the people who would decide whether we would be granted permission to apply for adoption. We still had a long way to go, but every success achieved along the way was cause for celebration.

It was a little unsettling to imagine a complete stranger reviewing all of our personal information. The silver lining was that, at this point, there was nothing for me to do but obsessively wonder what was transpiring in a little government office on the other side of the world. I wondered if they would like how we sounded on paper. Or perhaps they would decide we needed to supply more documents. We were promised a response within ten days after receiving our package. That meant we had ten full days ahead of us without having to pay anyone for anything. We took small comfort in this.

With child-like anticipation, I phoned our power of attorney in Ukraine on Day 10. With this phone call, I would discover if our documents satisfied the authorities' strict and continually evolving requirements or if we needed to supply more information. An acceptance on the first try would be considered quite a miracle. In all innocence, I thought we might be the exception. I hoped the answer on the other end would be, "Come on down—you are the next contestant on the Ukrainian adoption game!" My hopes were dashed as the answer at the other end was not very encouraging.

The most concerning feedback was that the Ukrainian officials did not like the appearance of our legalized documents. Either there were not enough stamps for their comfort, or the stamps were not big enough. I was not yet accustomed to the broken English of our power of attorney, Natasha, and so strained to understand what *exactly* was wrong with our rubber stamps. Although it may sound like a trivial issue, I was acutely aware that there was no Option B. Nobody but the Ukrainian embassy in Ottawa was authorized to legalize our adoption documents, and so if their procedure was not acceptable to the Ukrainian government, our story would end here.

Personally, I thought the package was quite attractive. It was carefully stapled together and covered with very official-looking stamps. I later discovered that our Swiss friends' legalized package was literally sewn together with thread. I was sorry our package was not as aesthetically pleasing, but unfortunately, there was nothing I could do to change this situation. In the end, the Ukrainian officials decided to accept our plain package. I think it was just an opportunity to make me squirm. And squirm I did until they finally agreed to review the information. The Ukrainian adoption officials asked us a few minor questions through Natasha and also requested three further documents. It seemed innocuous at the time, but one of these additional reports was almost enough to abort the entire project.

The first one was easy. They merely wanted a copy of the license held by the social worker who had performed our home study. That sounded reasonable enough. Other than the fact that each of these additional documents had to be translated, legalized, and couriered to Kiev, this was a relatively simple assignment. Besides, our translator needed a matching car for his wife. I dreaded breaking the news to Dave that the second additional document required us to undergo further bloodwork to test for specific communicable diseases. That was not the worst part. It was the third document that proved the most difficult. What we needed was a letter from our government stating that Katja would have full rights and privileges after she entered Canada. It didn't sound particularly complicated, but up until this point, I was still blissfully unacquainted with Immigration Canada. That was all about to change.

I found out about these documents on December 22, and so we could do nothing until the festive season passed. We had already waited six months to reach this stage so what difference could another couple of weeks make? I tried to put it out of my mind while we visited our families in Western Canada for the holidays. We would return to Montreal in the first week of January to quickly gather and courier the documents.

The Great Ice Storm

When we returned to Montreal on January 5, I planned to hit the pavement running in order to rapidly complete these last three documents the Ukrainian government required. What started on that day and lasted for the next several weeks could not have been predicted by anyone. We faced the beginning of what journalists would aptly name The Great Ice Storm.

I would not wish to pretend that bad winter weather in Canada is particularly shocking. In this case, what was shocking was the aftermath. Over a period of two days, parts of southern Ontario and Quebec received an amount of rainfall that usually falls over a span of two years. Compounding the amount of precipitation was the fact that temperatures hovered around zero degrees Celsius, so the rain fell in the form of ice pellets. If it had been colder, which is usually the case in Quebec in early January, the ice rain would have been light, fluffy, and relatively harmless snow. Under such conditions, we may have been slightly inconvenienced if we were trapped in our house by an enormous snowbank. That would have been favourable to what we experienced.

The ice rain beautifully coated all of the trees with frost as thick as an outstretched hand in some places. Benches were completely covered in shiny layers of ice and all walking surfaces had transformed into natural skating rinks. So far, it merely sounds like a photographer's paradise. It was not the actual storm that wreaked havoc on our adoption progress. The problems began when those beautiful, and very heavy, ice-covered branches became broken branches that fell on top of power lines. These lifelines to electricity snapped like twigs under the weight and fell to the ground to form heaps of useless, twisted metal. Within days, countless power lines and towers had been destroyed by the thick ice. As the ice rain continued to fall, the blackout region spread. At the height of the storm, three million people in Montreal and surrounding area were stranded without power, including us.

During that week, we tried to survive in our home with no heating source until we surrendered and found one of the few remaining unoccupied hotel rooms left in the city. To satisfy our hunger, we participated in some urban hunting, which required finding restaurants that miraculously had power. Often, the lights would flicker in the crowded restaurants and the entire clientele would cheer when they came back on. Producing our final three adoption-related documents would have to temporarily take a backseat to such activities as finding batteries, flashlights, firewood, and candles.

The experience was really quite remarkable. To see a normally vibrant North American city turn completely dark and quiet on a Friday afternoon was eerie. To watch our neighbourhood become pitch black and deserted before 5 p.m., was also strange. Most of all, to not know when it was ever going to end was extremely daunting. Little by little over the coming weeks, the city regained its power. We were fortunate that our neighbourhood was reconnected after eight days in the dark.

As a result of the storm, the entire Greater Montreal Area came to a dead halt for approximately a week. After the first week, the power that was restored to some parts of the city was only a fraction of what was normally required to feed its energy needs. Therefore, government officials urged businesses to remain closed for at least an additional week in order to conserve energy. For some, this meant an unexpected vacation. The initial one-week delay stretched out into several weeks.

After we had returned to our warm and lit home, all I could selfishly think about was that each person who could help me further our adoption project was shut out of their office. Little could be accomplished in these weeks. Much to Dave's dismay, we were still able to arrange our blood tests during this stage, as I will share more fully. Our patience was tested as our plans to wrap up the whole adoption in January regressed to a hope to complete the documents before the end of February.

One could never predict that a provincial state of emergency would erupt just as an adoption procedure reaches a critical stage. However, unexpected surprises should be included as part of a generic adoption checklist so that once you reach a roadblock, you will not be disappointed. Whew! What a relief to have completed the Unexpected Delay steps! At least we could be thankful that our Unexpected Delay was so dramatic that it somewhat distracted us from the fact that our adoption plans were temporarily suspended.

Once more lights started to come back on, I began simultaneously booking our flights, transportation, lodging arrangements, travel visas, and preparing Katja's room. The last weeks leading to our first trip to Ukraine were filled with a level of stress I had only ever imagined before. But first, those troublesome documents needed to be addressed. We weren't going anywhere until they were completed.

Eventually, everyone returned to work. The first stop was our social worker, where it was a relatively routine procedure to obtain a copy of her professional license. Recall that our second assignment was to obtain further blood test results. As predicted, Dave was less than enthusiastic about this one. I recognize he is not the only male who could easily faint at the mere thought of an attack by a killer needle. You would think these needles are the size of a missile the way they carry on about it. Come on, guys, buck up—it will hurt the needle more than it will hurt you!

Ironically, we were undergoing fertility testing while we completed the latter stages of gathering these documents. We had just recently endured the trauma of blood tests as part of that process, but Dave's results inexplicably disappeared. I dreaded breaking the news to him that he had to return for an additional round of bloodwork to satisfy the adoption requirements, as it had been difficult to coax him to the hospital the first time. After some pleading on my part, the hospital staff promised to take enough samples to satisfy the fertility and adoption requirements simultaneously. I thought this was good news.

Even though these blood tests would solve both of our problems in one fell swoop, Dave was at the point of fighting the Ukrainian government in order to convince them we should not have to take these tests on the grounds that the information was none of their business in the first place. This was his defense. I envisioned the entire project disintegrating because of this needle. I tried my hardest to convince Dave that he would survive the ordeal . . . again. All I knew for certain was there was no way the Ukrainian government would acquiesce on this point. Fortunately, Dave conquered his fears enough to brave yet another round of blood tests.

I could sense his growing tension as we neared the hospital that day and then had to wait anxiously in the waiting room until our number was called. I can only imagine what thoughts passed through his mind to create such angst about a needle. In his defense, I must say that Dave managed quite well, although at one point his colouring made the pasty eggshell hospital walls look like a vibrant hue in comparison. I pleaded with the doctor to ensure the results would not disappear again, as I was certain this would be our last chance at this step. I concluded that it is good for the human race that men were originally built to be the hunters of food and not the bearers of children.

Dave's stress for this step focused on the few seconds of a needle penetrating his skin. All I had to do, on the other hand, was arrange the tests, convince Dave we should continue to the hospital while the city was in a state of crisis, and arrange the documentation of the results to be prepared and then sent to the Ukrainian government. Oh, yeah, and I had to endure a killer needle also. I am happy to report that we both survived the hospital visit.

By this point, I was a seasoned document gatherer and acutely aware that the translator charged for his services by the word. Therefore, it was important that each document be as short and concise as possible. In order to obtain a document that we could afford to translate, I drafted a letter for the hospital to emulate. Basically, I wanted a letter that said: Michele—no AIDS or syphilis; Dave—ditto.

Unfortunately, the letter I received was dense with information. It started with "Please refer to the attached reports showing the results of . . ." followed by four attached reports, each containing approximately 1,000 words. Panic set in as I saw the cost of the translation in my head. We were well beyond buying him a luxury car with these documents. With these, he could retire on his yacht while sunning himself on his private island. After a brief anxiety attack, I managed to overcome the problem by highlighting the few words I really needed to be translated on each page. Hopefully this would be acceptable to the authorities in Ukraine; it was worth a shot.

So that left us with the third document on our list. It all seemed innocent enough at the outset when the Ukrainian officials requested a letter stating that, if we were given permission to adopt a child, he or she would be allowed into Canada and given the status of a permanent resident. Although it sounded logical to me, I could not find anyone who would write this letter for me. The most frustrating aspect was that some friends in Switzerland, who had adopted from the same orphanage a mere month earlier, had not required this document. There was no way we would ever convince the Ukrainian government to remove this requirement, so we had no choice but to plead with various government departments in our own country to write such a letter. Nobody was willing to do it.

In the process, I held many discussions with staff from various government departments. My personal favourite was my inaugural call with Immigration Canada. I clearly explained the short and simple letter we needed. The woman on the other end promptly informed me this would not be possible. When I asked why, she replied it could not be done because such a letter had never been written before. For a moment, I felt sympathy for this woman who worked a job in which she could never be allowed to think creatively. I mean, imagine that your whole day is filled entirely and exclusively with repetitive actions and procedures that have already been done—no original words, thoughts, or actions allowed.

After this brief moment of sympathy for this and all other civil servants, I remembered my own sad story. I pleaded with her to circumvent the normal procedure just this once, as we needed it for our adoption case and there was no way around it. She reassured me that I should not worry, as we would automatically receive such a letter after we had successfully passed through the Ukrainian court system. Apparently, this was a process that had occurred before. I tried to mask my frustration when I reiterated there would be no court proceedings if we could not get the permission to adopt a child from that country, and the Ukrainians would not give us permission until I could send them this letter!

This circular conversation continued, and I received every answer from "we don't do that here" to "in twenty-two years I have never seen such a letter." Finally, in desperation, I asked what would happen if we would arrive at the Montreal airport with our new daughter. Would she be let into the country? "Of course," was the answer. All I needed was for someone to write that answer on paper and so I thought we had made some progress until she reverted back to "I cannot do that letter for you because it has never been done before."

There were several moments throughout the adoption procedure that I questioned why we ever started and if we would ever win the battle. This was one of those times. There seemed to be no way out of this dilemma, and so in my frustration, I did what any mature and professional adult would do. I hung up the phone.

After I regained my composure, I telephoned Natasha to inform her I could not seem to get this document. So, she pleaded with the Ukrainian government workers to make an exception to this new rule so we would not be required to supply the letter. Although she tried her best to relieve us of this problem, the Ukrainian officials would not listen to our pleas. The bottom line was that we needed this letter or else had to let go of our vision. That was not an option.

A sudden burst of inspiration turned me toward the one person within the Quebec government administration who had been a tremendous help to me up to that point—a woman I will refer to as Marie from the *Secrétariat à l'adoption internationale*. Within minutes of sending an urgent message that outlined my request, Marie phoned me to say that of course she would write this letter without delay. This was one of the many times she went over and above her job description to help us. I cannot thank Marie enough for all the work she did for us. I only wished she also worked at the Department of Immigration. If you are setting out to complete your adoption independently, I highly recommend finding people who can see your vision and therefore will champion your cause through creative and bold actions. Don't be afraid to ask these supporters for help as you may need them.

Without delay, Marie prepared the letter and the precious document was ready for pick-up the very next day. It was 4 p.m. on a Friday—one of the busiest traffic hours of the week at the best of times, further compounded by the fact that Montreal was in the middle of a vicious snowstorm. At least it was snow instead of ice. It did not matter, as nothing was keeping me from this letter. I inched the car toward Marie's office in the blizzard, found a parking spot that wasn't overtaken by a snow drift, and then trudged through thigh-high snowbanks to retrieve the letter. The rest of the staff had left early to brave the stormy highways, but she was there to greet me with a smile and what I'd come for. I was so relieved to see her and this piece of paper.

The next and last stop on that blustery winter day was the office of the translator. I snuck in within moments of the office closing for the week and was promised I would be able to pick up the documents the following Thursday at noon. Scheduling was critical at this point as we had just a short window to forward the three documents to the Ukrainian authorities before they would close our file and we would have to reapply. This thought was never far from my mind, as well as the fact that, after I retrieved the translated documents, they would still have to be rubber-stamped by the Ukrainian embassy in Ottawa. I thought I'd done a good job of conveying the critical nature of the timing in this case.

As I neared the city the following Thursday afternoon to retrieve the translated copy of the documents, my phone rang. I was leery when I heard a Ukrainian accent on the other end. My suspicions turned out to be warranted as I was informed that the documents would not be ready for me on that day. At the very least, this news was annoying, as the city skyline was already in sight when I received the call. Far worse than that, though, were the implications on our adoption of Katja.

Every lost day meant our travel plans were further delayed. We were targeting a specific departure date to meet the regulatory requirements. The deadline was already very tight, so a delay of one or two days could prevent us from reaching it. Again, I reverted to foolproof methods to get my own way. I begged and pleaded to receive my translations that day.

From the translator's viewpoint, I probably seemed a demanding and unreasonable customer. At that point, I did not care though. These people stood in the way of us reaching our daughter. I pictured myself trampling over them if I had to. Miraculously, the translations were suddenly completed on that day. In the end, I think the translator and his staff were just happy to be done with me.

I remember being asked, well after Katja was safely home with us, what would have made the process easier to endure. At times of frustration like I felt at this particular moment, I considered that if we did not have a specific child in mind, the delays would not have been so difficult to endure. On the other hand, this was where having a clear vision was critical.

It was imagining Katja in the orphanage each additional day, week, month that fueled my motivation even though it simultaneously magnified the frustration levels. Had we not had a specific child in mind, we may not have had enough stamina to endure the various challenges we encountered. When frustrations set in, it is helpful to go back and reread Chapter Two to rediscover one's motivation to adopt. With this in mind, these setbacks become mere inconveniences towards realizing a vision.

Immigration Procedures

My initial call with the Department of Immigration foreshadowed our next setback and plot twist, as this government body became the next antagonist in our story. Canadian immigration requirements for form-filling and money-paying must be met on both the federal and provincial levels. The process is quite complex, and it is extremely helpful to complete the paperwork as much as possible from the comforts of home rather than from within your adopted child's birth country.

The Canadian embassy in Kiev required the following four documents before they could issue a child's visa:

1. Standard administrative forms obtained and completed in advance. This stage was uncharacteristically easy.

2. Passport with child's new name (after the court proceedings are finalized). Once the adoption was completed in Ukraine, this document would be relatively painless to obtain.

3. A letter from the Quebec government stating the child

would be allowed into the country. At the last minute, I was able to obtain this document from my usual source, Marie.

4. Medical reports of the child. This was by far the most difficult step in the immigration process. We didn't know it at the time, but the results from this step would block us from bringing Katja home after her adoption.

In order to fulfill this last requirement, Katja had to be examined by one of four doctors on a list of acceptable Ukrainian doctors. Two of these doctors were in Kiev. From North American standards, a requirement to visit a doctor a mere two hours away would seem like a menial errand, but when wrapped up as part of an international adoption, logistics can get complicated very rapidly.

From our kitchen table in Montreal, I arranged for Katja to be released from the orphanage, hired Natasha to accompany her—and obtained the permissions required to do so, hired a driver for the day, and scheduled an appointment with one of the two certified doctors. That was the easy part. We hoped that Katja, who had only been released from the orphanage twice in the first forty months of her life for two major and painful surgeries, would respond well to the unknown doctor who would poke and prod her. This outcome was by no means a sure thing, but we had no choice but to make the necessary arrangements.

One problem we encountered at this stage was courtesy of our government officials stationed in Ukraine, who informed us that Katja could not undergo these tests until we were physically present and after we had received official permission to adopt her. This completely contradicted the story I had been told by the Canadian immigration experts at home, who'd said they could be done ahead of time. Oh, you have to love bureaucracy! I mean, where else can you simultaneously receive two completely opposite answers to the same question?

Before continuing, here is where I will reinforce another life lesson that is directly related to the need to have a vision and why I am dragging you through this difficult time. Sprinkled throughout the pages of this book are examples of when people told us we couldn't do something. As mentioned previously, as long as an action does not contravene any laws or moral code, it may be that someone else thinks what you are setting out to do is impossible because they have never seen it before. The word *vision* itself is quite interesting as one of its meanings requires seeing with one's eyes an object that is present before them, while a different meaning requires imagining something that does not yet exist. It is this latter skill that we attribute to people we characterize as visionaries. Be patient with those who lack the imagination to see your vision before it materializes, but don't let them take yours away.

So now let's go back to our adoption and our immigration friends, who would not allow for Katja's medical tests to occur until we were physically present to take her. This obstacle led to another 3 a.m. phone call with the Canadian embassy in Kiev, during which I once again pleaded and begged for permission for Natasha to complete this step prior to our arrival in Ukraine. Sometimes, I think this pleading and begging approach is underrated. Contrary to what I had been told days before, we did receive the permissions required and so we could stroke another potential obstacle off the list.

Natasha graciously scheduled a day off work to complete this fourteen-hour mission for us. I knew the schedule they were following and could think of little else that day. With each passing hour, I was busy trying to determine what was happening at that moment. From thousands of miles away, I stalked Natasha's house with my repeated phone calls, as I was anxious for any report. I passed the time speaking with her daughter multiple times, hoping Natasha would return home if I just stayed on the line a few extra minutes.

At the end of the day, Natasha did walk through her apartment door to be greeted by me on the phone. She recounted the long and difficult day she had endured at the hands of Immigration Canada. Not surprisingly, Katja was extremely nervous when she was plucked from the only home she had ever known by a stranger, to be driven by another stranger to a strange place where she would be examined by a strange doctor. It is important to keep in mind that Katja's life to that point had been very structured and predictable. Anything out of the regular routine would have been a cause of concern for her.

We were relieved as we believed that Katja would only have to endure this once. Instead, Natasha was informed during the appointment that they would have to return, as Katja would also have to be examined by specialists, including a psychologist. So, we repeated exactly the same plan the following week so that Katja could be subjected to more confusing and stressful doctor appointments. From my perspective, I was relieved that these tests were conducted at this point, because I thoroughly believed this was our final battle. It had been a long war, but it looked like we had finally won.

Following these two rushed doctor examinations in Kiev, some forms we believed to be routine summarized the test results and were sent to Vienna for analysis by a doctor who never met Katja and who did not even share a common language with the doctors who'd written the reports. Somehow, this procedure was meant to accurately depict Katja's physical and mental state at the time.

There were two issues working against us. If you are a parent, I presume you are aware of the phenomenon that can transform your perfect little angel-child into an unknown alien as soon as you require them to perform for a stranger, including doctors. No matter how confident and well-adjusted they are in regular circumstances, they may not be in the mood to behave as they normally would.

As I write this section, I think back to an experience with our then-three-year-old twins. On this particular day we were going on a little field trip to Walmart for Christmas photos. Earlier that morning, I was so relieved when they began their days in upbeat moods and even practiced their cutest smiles for their private audience of Mama at home. Even while I parked the vehicle at the mall, they were excited for this new adventure. Then we entered the photo studio. Instantly, I had one little boy wrapped around my leg crying and the other balking about even entering the room. Through playing, singing, and dancing in the middle of the store, I managed to squeeze just enough smiles out of them for the photographer to get some great shots. Of course, as soon as we left the studio, they were co-operative and full of smiles once again.

Although I had thoroughly prepared our toddlers for this experience, it took great effort to elicit a positive response from them and it was only because their mom was with them that it was a success. If a stranger had just whisked them off by surprise from home and driven them two hours away in a strange car to visit strange doctors, I suspect that they, too, would have completely underperformed.

Likewise, it should not have surprised any of the medical professionals that Katja was unresponsive to this new doctor in Kiev. She had no way of knowing that this stranger was in a position to determine her future and that she therefore needed to respond positively to him. Instead of giving her the benefit of the doubt, the doctor wrote an extremely unfavourable report about Katja. His theory was that perhaps Katja exhibited signs of fetal alcohol syndrome. Although this was proven wrong over the coming months, once the words were inked on paper, they could not be retracted, and Canadian Immigration took them to be fact as opposed to a hypothesis yet to be proven.

I had hoped that Katja's bilateral cleft lip and palate would not create another obstacle to her immigration proceedings. After all, in Canada approximately one child in 750 is born with this condition, while in Ukraine the rate is considerably higher, at one in 450. Nobody knows for certain what causes the condition, but what is known in the era of modern medicine is that the treatment is relatively routine, and a complete restoration is available through plastic surgery.

Most North American children born with a cleft lip and/or palate begin treatments within the first couple of months of their lives. Katja, on the other hand, did not have any proper work performed on her palate until she was already three years old, and then only due to the generous intervention of Hope Now. Katja knew she looked different than the other children and therefore was reticent to look others in the eye. As well, she did not have the ability to communicate effectively with anyone verbally. The workers at the orphanage had never heard her speak to this point. It was not surprising that she did not respond well to the questions posed by the doctors. This did not go unnoticed and so her cleft lip and palate received dishonourable mention as well.

Other than being subjected to the occasional plastic surgery, orthodontic work, and intensive speech therapy, overall Katja proved to be remarkably healthy. At the time, we did not know the extent of the care Katja would require. We were still shocked to discover that the doctor in Vienna rejected Katja for immigration simply due to her lack of response at the doctor appointments. The conclusion was that our daughter would create too much of a burden on the Canadian taxpayer.

The results of these medical visits did not reach us until we were already in Ukraine preparing for our court date. It was fortuitous that we did not receive them sooner, as we would have been discouraged to learn that we had an enormous and unexpected obstacle ahead as a result. Instead, we just continued to inch closer to our vision by tackling one hurdle at a time.

While Katja was undergoing these medical tests, there was more work to be done on the ground in Canada. Sooner or later, I had to endure the procedures that every immigrant must endure within our own country and what an eye-opener it turned out to be. I quickly learned that in order to earn the privilege of waiting in a room with a couple hundred other potential immigrants, I had to first pay my fees and take a number. Upon entering the dimly lit institution, I observed how odd it was to see a waiting room full of people, all sitting in chairs that faced the same way, staring at the ceiling. Once I caught on to the procedure, I understood I was required to wait anxiously for my number to appear on the screen, which was conveniently hung at neck-craning height from the high ceiling above us.

There I sat—a visible minority in my country of birth. After what seemed like an eternity, my number popped up on the screen and so I was at last invited to mount the decrepit back stairs to the required floor. Imagine my relief to see that now I was only waiting in a line of fifty people. My patience paid off when it was finally my turn to be let into the back offices.

I give credit to the people who work in these offices. In fact, after this trip, I was slightly more forgiving of all immigration workers I had ever spoken with over the phone. If I had to work in such a bleak building, my character would likely be affected. The cubicles in which the workers sat paralleled the rigidity of the work procedures themselves. As for the work itself, their days were spent helping people, who were often coming from difficult circumstances, complete complex processes that may be life-altering.

My goal was simple and that was to just fill out whatever forms they threw at me and do anything else they told me to do. The whole experience only took a few hours, but it felt much longer. There was nothing particularly unpleasant about the task, but I recall feeling a sense of relief when I emerged from that building and felt the bright sunshine on my face.

By this point, we had completed those additional three documents the Ukrainian government required. Now that I was a pro at this document stage, everything was translated, legalized, and sent to Ukraine within a couple of weeks. We managed to open Katja's immigration file and had all of the papers we would need to bring her home. Despite the trouble we'd caused the Ukrainian government, they decided to allow us into their country to adopt one of their children. We were home free! We dared to think that all we had to do was fly to Ukraine, fill out some more forms, show up at court, and then bring our daughter home.

The extent to which travel is required to complete the adoption process depends entirely on the birth country of the child. Some countries do not require the presence of the adoptive parents. To satisfy the Ukrainian adoption official requirements, both Dave and I had to be present for all steps right up to the actual court hearing. I have heard successful adoption stories of parents whose new child was delivered to them. Although this simplifies logistics, we appreciated having the opportunity to experience Katja's heritage personally.

Our brief sojourn in Ukraine was enough to gain invaluable

snippets of information regarding the care Katja had received to that point and how she responded to certain situations. We have also been able to share a bit with her about her initial home through photos and personal memories. She loves to hear our stories about our time with her in Cherkasy. If possible, I recommend that you do not miss this opportunity. It is such an important and fascinating experience.

So now that the documents were nearing completion, my focus shifted to our travel preparations. As we had previously lived overseas, we had travelled to a variety of countries in the years preceding the adoption. Although we generally felt prepared for travelling to Ukraine, I was a little disturbed when we were encouraged to include toilet paper on our packing list. I took great comfort when assured that hot water would be readily available.

Do Not Forget the Gifts

I love Christmas. I enjoy giving gifts to people and seeing their reaction when I have selected that special something just for them. Similarly, I was excited to present gifts to Natasha and all the other kind people in Ukraine who had helped so much to make our dream come true. What I could not reconcile though were the multitude of gifts—in the form of money, chocolates, or perfume—we were strongly encouraged to bring for the officials, who could easily stop our adoption if they didn't like us enough.

I would be interested to see the reaction of Canadian officials, particularly immigration officers, if I brought them presents to encourage them to process our file a little faster. At best, I would have been mocked for my strange behaviour. At worst, I would have been arrested for attempted bribery. It seemed a bit unorthodox to bring gifts to help grease the Ukrainian adoption wheels, but we did as we were told. Our first trip occurred shortly after Valentine's Day, so at least I was able to profit from sales on perfume and chocolates.

We were informed that the women prefer cosmetic items, but balk at scented soaps, as they are considered lower-quality gifts. For the men I stuck with chocolate and, of course, US cash was always welcome. Once we actually arrived in Ukraine and met the various parties who were working to make our adoption dreams come true, the gift-giving became instantly more palatable. In most cases, the people toiling for us really had made a concerted effort to speed up our adoption process. The presents were often a payment for the overtime hours people were required to work to ensure our adoption was completed within a short period. Furthermore, as hard as it is hard to imagine, the average monthly wage at the time was not much more than what Dave and I spent weekly at the movie theatre after buying popcorn and drinks.

The other interesting observation was that the people who received our gifts all seemed genuinely embarrassed to take something from us. They almost appeared to be surprised at the gesture. We knew this was all part of the game, as they themselves had already suggested to Natasha what they would like us to bring for them. However, their traits of humility and graciousness throughout the whole process were remarkable.

So many related events occur simultaneously in preparation for the adoption itself that make the corresponding travel required much more complex than a typical vacation or business trip. There are many more items on the To Do list than usual, including packing all of the adoption and travel related documentation as well as food and clothing for your new child. Oh, yeah, and don't forget the toilet paper.

Dave and Michele – on their honeymoon as a new married couple

Dave and Michele visiting Katja at The House of Babies, Cherkasy Ukraine

*Michele and Katja return to The House of Babies
after a walk with Katja's cohort*

*Michele and Katja on Adoption Day!
The fight to bring Katja home would start very soon.*

Dave and Katja leaving Ukraine to start her new life in Canada

Michele celebrates her first Mother's Day with Katja

Katja quickly conquers her fear of water

Matthew and Nicholas come home from the hospital

Katja loves her new brothers

Katja continues to dote on Matthew and Nicholas

Matthew and Nicholas are happy babies

Michele and the kids – early years

Returning to Montreal after visiting family in Saskatchewan –
Lake Superior, Ontario

The whole family – 2003

Katja revisits her heritage through Ukrainian dancing lessons

Sports have always played an important role in the twins' lives

Current day – Katja in Banff, Alberta

*Current day – Proud mom with Nicholas and Matthew
after a basketball game*

The family is now complete with Chloe

Chapter Seven

Dobroye Dyen, Ukraine!

inally, the paper chase was complete, and I could not believe that the highly anticipated day had actually arrived. We were on an airplane flying to Ukraine to meet and adopt our daughter, whom we had come to know and love through two-dimensional photos and documents.

We landed in Kiev mid-afternoon on a sunny Monday in early spring, at 3 p.m. to be exact, with the ambitious plan to obtain permission to adopt from the federal level before the close of the business day so we could reach our final destination of Cherkasy that same evening. After receiving authorization at the federal level, we would then have to prove ourselves to local authorities in Cherkasy in order to be cleared to adopt a child from that region. Then, after we received local permissions, a court date would be granted, and only then could we complete the final paperwork regarding our new daughter's immigration to Canada.

We were well aware of this tight sequence of events and were determined to clear each one successfully and on our carefully contrived schedule. As another 200 kilometres lay between us and

Cherkasy, we hoped we would not need to return to Kiev until we were ready to fly back to Canada.

Within moments of our arrival in the Kiev Boryspil Airport, we had our first up close and personal glimpse of the Ukrainian authorities' passion for paperwork and their precious stamps. Simply conquering the passport control line took almost a full hour, as everyone who passed through was required to produce a series of official documents before entering the baggage claim area. Each paper was checked and rechecked. Several unfortunate souls ahead of us endured extensive questioning when they presented their visas. I was a little nervous to approach the desk when our number was called. Surprisingly, we slipped through without any hassles. Whew! So far, so good.

Suddenly, my thoughts shifted to the arrival of our luggage or lack thereof. Under normal circumstances, reclaiming lost luggage is annoying, as its retrieval typically requires extra time spent waiting in line, filling out forms, and living without a change of clothes or toothbrush for a few days. In our current situation, lost luggage would have caused more than routine irritation. Don't forget that we had packed gifts valued in the hundreds of dollars that, we were warned, could go missing if they landed in the wrong hands. If our presents disappeared, our adoption schedule would potentially be moved to the slow track.

For these reasons, I was exceptionally happy and relieved when I spotted our familiar luggage waiting for us. We had lugged along three huge suitcases, as well as four carry-on bags. In addition to the gifts, we'd also brought clothes and toys for our daughter in the hopes that we would need them for the return voyage. We claimed our luggage and walked through the doors that led to an austere waiting room. We were ready to greet the country in its entirety.

My heart skipped when I spotted our names written on a

homemade cardboard sign. I knew Natasha was on the other end of the sign and I was so pleased to finally meet her face to face. She and Vladimir #1—I will explain a bit later—greeted us warmly. Without further delays, we headed immediately to the adoption centre in Kiev.

General Reaction to Ukraine

For us, much of our ten-day first trip to Ukraine was a whirlwind of appointments, but some points are lucid enough for me to share them with you today. Part of the lack of clarity is due to the instinctual survival technique I employ whenever I encounter stressful situations in that I consciously desensitize myself to my surroundings. At the same time, I wanted to fully experience the beautiful country that was home to our future daughter. I will share some of my observations upfront to help set the stage for the next ten days.

We had experienced culture shock before in our many travels, but nothing really prepared us for the widespread poverty in this former Communist country. Sadly, with the introduction of democracy had come a drastic increase in crime and corruption, resulting in escalating poverty. We had visited comparatively poor countries before, but on those trips we had stayed in resorts for tourists, and therefore had been comfortably numbed to the conditions faced by most of the local residents. Our Egyptian vacation suddenly comes to mind. Our beautiful hotel was an oasis in the midst of Cairo's dirt and poverty.

Although Ukraine was a country where many faced economic hardships, it was also home to some of the most generous people I have ever been privileged to meet. Our host family, as well as those we met in their inner circle of friends and family, were extremely warm-hearted and remarkable people. Even with the language barrier, I managed to share some good laughs with our unilingual Ukrainian hostess, Vera. Her teenage son was often around to help translate for us, but if not, we found a means to communicate.

Once we began to familiarize ourselves with the Ukrainian customs, we became more comfortable in our surroundings. Daily, we passed rows of elderly women who were selling a few jars of pickles and several apples from the top of an old cardboard box, desperate for someone to come and be their next customer. The apples were often so bruised that they would not have made it to our store shelves, but the Ukrainians were adept at not wasting food. We were reminded of this at every meal, as we witnessed how every table scrap was saved and then used for the next meal. This was an eye-opener for us. The culinary experience was especially difficult for Dave's discriminating (he does not like when I say fussy) appetite, although he was thrilled to discover upon our return home that he had lost ten pounds!

Speaking of Dave, I am sure he will never forget our experiences at the market. First, I must introduce you to our main driver, Vladimir #2. About that—we had three different drivers throughout the entire ordeal, and all three were named Vladimir! Vladimir #1 picked us up from the airport on our first trip, but it was Vladimir #2 who was with us on a daily basis. On our second trip, neither #1 nor #2 was available to pick us up from the airport, so Natasha arranged for another driver. I kid you not—Vladimir #3 was hired for our second trip. Anyway, back to the market as we continue to set the stage for our time in Ukraine.

After a particularly grueling day of fighting bureaucracy, we asked Vladimir #2 to stop at the market so Dave could buy something familiar to eat. I waited in the car with Vladimir with great anticipation, as I could only imagine what Dave would find to satisfy his hunger. He came back empty-handed, but with a shocked expression on his face. It was difficult for him to put his reaction into words. I pressed in though, as I had never seen Dave react to a situation in this strange way. He regained his composure and relayed to us that he had seen a boar's head displayed for sale. The head sat in a bowl with its face pointing upwards and two eyes pleading with passers-by to invite him to their home for dinner. We discovered later that it is common to boil the head to make boar's head jelly.

Before every meal that followed that experience, Dave would ask me in French from across the table what he was eating, for fear the boar's head had found its way to his plate. One day, we had fish for dinner and Dave was nervous as the fish head was carefully placed in the fridge for future use. The next day I thought I would have a little fun at my husband's expense so when he nodded to the food on the table and asked "Qu'est-ce que c'est?" I couldn't resist responding, "Poisson!"

The outdoor market was a wonderful place to directly experience the daily lives of the locals. We tagged along with our host family on a crisp Saturday afternoon to the main market in Cherkasy, which was a city of approximately 300,000 people. It appeared as though tradition dictated every citizen attend one of the three big markets in the city on Saturday, which each consisted of row upon row of adjoining tents. In each tent a vendor almost begged us to buy his goods, especially upon discovering we were Canadian. I was genuinely surprised by the high quality of the clothes available for purchase. Had I not been so modest, I may have dared to try on a new wardrobe. However, the only change room available was a makeshift human wall created by whoever happened to be standing around at the time. I saved my dollars that day.

On the weekend we were also privileged to attend our hosts'

church. I was informed that married women were expected to cover their hair and wear long skirts, but I had nothing suitable in my three large suitcases and four carry-on bags. Vera reassured me, though, when she smiled and in very broken English communicated that what I wore was OK for me, not for them. Once we were at the service, we did not understand a word that was spoken but the singing was beautiful, and everyone greeted us with a warm smile.

Most of our cultural activities were saved for the weekend, as we spent our time during the week sequestered in government and administration buildings. Many of these buildings would have been condemned in North America. I was surprised to learn that some of them were actually quite new, but they were slapped together with cheap materials in order to make some quick and easy rent money. Also, ongoing maintenance of buildings was considered a luxury expense many landlords could not afford.

Each large concrete cubic structure we entered offered the same atmosphere, complete with accompanying stale smells. Buildings were built to be functional and not for aesthetic appeal. We were cautious when we opened a new door, as we were never too confident what might be around the next corner. If we were lucky to find unbroken chairs in the long corridors, we passed most of our time sitting in them, awaiting our next meeting. All buildings were dimly lit and sparsely, if at all, decorated. In the absence of any interesting scenery, our favourite hobby soon became people-watching. We were treated to a never-ending supply of subjects to observe as the workers made their way from one closed door to another, which leads me to another trivial observation.

The concept of an open-door policy was definitely lacking in Ukraine. Each employee seemed to have a separate office and each office was accessed through a heavy door that remained closed until someone passed through it. All doors made a terrific slam when shut. If that weren't enough, this annoying sound reverberated as it echoed its way down the long hallway. It appeared as though people passed their working days entering and leaving offices—never forgetting the obligatory door slam behind them. Sometimes a worker carried a piece of paper, seemingly to legitimize another slam of a colleague's door. The workers were well-trained to carry out this tradition without ever letting go of a very serious frown on their faces.

We shadowed Natasha around from office to office, corridor to corridor, and closed door to closed door. When it was finally our turn to slam the door behind us, that meant we were meeting another crucial contact on our adoption journey. On several occasions we arrived at a prescheduled meeting to discover our intended host was simply absent. Furthermore, nobody could tell us if or when the intended party would reappear behind the heavy door. Being stood up, compounded by the acceptance and almost expectation of this occurrence, was disturbing to two time-obsessed Westerners. Inherent in the Ukrainian way of life were many hours spent waiting, and for us this was not easy. But wait we did, over and over again.

We were not the only ones who were forced to wait. Our faithful Vladimirs catered to our schedule. The fraction of time we spent in a moving vehicle was insignificant compared to the hours spent waiting inside. No matter how long we were held captive in one of the countless buildings, our chauffeur awaited us when we escaped. It likely helped the Vladimirs to pass the time knowing that we paid the equivalent of one month's salary for each day of driving . . . and waiting.

From our point of view, the convenience of a car dedicated to us was worth every penny paid to the Vladimirs. If doubts of this

were ever to creep in, we had to look no further than the perpetu-
ally crowded trolley buses to be convinced. We managed to build
a good relationship with Vladimir #2. This was not easy considering the immense language barrier. We had fun exchanging our
twenty words of mixed Russian and Ukrainian with his ten words
of broken English. No matter what we had just endured, Vladimir
always had his gold-toothed smile waiting for us.

Now that the scene is set, let's go back to that first day in Ukraine.
We had just landed at Kiev Boryspil Airport. Within moments of
leaving the airport, we would experience a taste of the Ukrainian
bureaucracy on which we would feast for the next ten days.

Our First Government Meeting

There was not much time left in the workday to receive the
required permissions from the federal authorities. We arrived at
the government building at 4 p.m., and we were hoping to finalize
the procedures before the office closed at 5 p.m., so we could head
right down to Cherkasy that same night. Customer service was not
the priority in these government departments. Nobody seemed
to mind if we were waiting without any communication from
the staff. Regular closing hours came and went, and we were still
waiting in our first corridor. In words we could not understand,
Natasha begged the people to see us that day as we did not have
anywhere to stay in Kiev.

Dave and I observed our surroundings to help distract us
from our predicament. It became immediately obvious to us
that such amenities as functioning lightbulbs, public washroom
facilities, and chairs for those forced to wait, were not considered
necessities. We were also introduced to the door-slamming and
paper-carrying rituals on this first day. Perhaps it was the thought

of us camped out on their doorsteps that finally led the workers to stay overtime on our behalf. Maybe they knew all along they would see us that day. If they did, they played their cards close to their chest as we certainly had no idea how this would play out.

Whatever the case, after an indeterminate period of time and well after closing hours, someone invited us through our first set of heavy, closed doors. Dave and I quietly took our seats and let Natasha go to work for us. Although we could not understand a word that was spoken, we could ascertain that Natasha was earnestly pleading with the workers to complete our documents that day. We will never know if it was Natasha's charm, or the chocolates and perfume we bestowed upon our hosts, but somehow we were promised our documents by the end of the evening.

Basically, what these people had to do for us was create a nice parcel out of all the original documents and translated versions I had couriered over the course of the last several months, along with the three additional reports we'd brought along with us. They literally used a needle and thread to sew through the fifty-odd-page package, and then add their own obligatory stamps and signatures. Painstakingly slow is the only way I can describe this step.

Dave and I sat in the office of what we assumed to be the manager while Natasha joined the workers in the mini sewing bee. We felt awkward as we sat idly in the office of this woman who spoke no English. She passed much of the time on what seemed like personal calls and reading the newspaper while we waited and waited. Perhaps she was explaining to her family that she was missing out on dinner because of these demanding Canadian strangers who'd showed up near the end of the day insisting their adoption documents be processed. At one point during a tentative conversation between Dave and myself, I became suspicious that she really could understand English perfectly. This was not the only time we questioned their perceived lack of linguistic competence. We realized it would be extremely convenient for them to pretend not to understand English in order to be privy to what we thought were private conversations. We played it safe and spoke only French in public.

After a long wait, our nice little package was assembled. It felt strange yet comforting to hold this beautifully bound bundle of documents I had couriered from Montreal some time before. It seemed like many months had passed since I last held those papers, when in reality it was only two months since I had tracked our package throughout Eastern Europe with the help of Mike, our friendly neighbourhood courier. We were elated with the results of this visit as we now had permission at the national level to adopt a Ukrainian child. It was 8 p.m. when we were released from the building and we just had one more stop before heading for Cherkasy.

Before we left Kiev that evening, we convinced Natasha and Vladimir that a stop at McDonald's would be a great dining option. We were all hungry and Dave and I were craving something familiar. The Golden Arches were like an oasis in a desert. Natasha and Vladimir informed us they would never eat at McDonald's because it was too expensive. It was our pleasure to treat all four adults to a full dinner for a total of approximately ten dollars.

It Was a Dark and Foggy Night . . .

On a night so thick with fog we literally could not see any road ahead of us, our very young Vladimir #1 raced toward Cherkasy on a winding, invisible road. I was terrified. When Dave admitted his fear as well, I knew this was serious as he typically tries to ease my anxiety by not admitting his own. This time, though, it was too difficult to deny the sense of danger. We had absolutely no way of knowing if a car was coming toward us or even if we were on the right side of the road. Normally, one slows down in these conditions, but not our driver. He insisted on driving at breakneck speed the whole way home.

I could not believe we had come this whole way and endured all that we had just to die in the backseat of this old car on some crooked little road between Kiev and Cherkasy. Thoughts of how our families would find out about our tragic demise raced through my head. In case our nerves were not completely raw, we were serenaded the whole way by loud, thumping techno music that pumped through crackling, tinny speakers.

Throughout our late-night dark and foggy journey, three different policemen pulled us over at what seemed like random checkpoints. The police stood by the edge of the road, waiting to wave an unsuspecting driver to the side with the use of a flashlight. Oddly enough, people actually stopped. The standard uniform of these law enforcers was a long grey coat, a fur hat, and a very serious facial expression. Dave and I were raised on a diet of American movies, and so naturally imagined we would be whisked away to a clandestine meeting with the KGB to be interrogated. I cannot say I was at all disappointed to discover they really were not interested in us personally. Another bright spot to these checkpoints was that the car was temporarily in park.

The officers merely wanted to check the car's contents and registration. Each time, our driver had to explain who was in the car and why we were transporting several enormous pieces of luggage. We learned that this form of questioning was standard procedure, but it was unnerving to us nonetheless. Later, we would realize that one of the leftovers from the Communist days was the rigorous attention to detail by all levels of authority. In order to maintain control over heavily populated regions, the former government had to offer as little freedom as possible and not make allowances for individual differences. Some of these practices carried over into the new and fragile democratic system.

Momentarily, it flashed through my mind that Katja would come from such a rigid environment that could only be compounded in an orphanage setting. I wondered if she would have problems adapting to our home, which would be filled with choices for her. How she would respond to such freedom remained to be seen. This was assuming, of course, that we made it alive through this drive to Cherkasy to meet and adopt her.

With massive sighs of relief, we arrived at our destination at 2 a.m., to discover that our gracious hosts had waited up to greet us. This was indicative of the Ukrainian hospitality we would encounter over the course of the next ten days. However, I must admit there was one family member I had difficulty warming up to, and that was Petrushka.

Petrushka was the family bird. He was free to fly around the small apartment all day long, until someone decided it was time for him to go in his cage for the night. Petrushka was harmless enough and so it was not really his fault he made my life difficult. The problem lay in my aversion to birds swooping at my head, and so I was not sure how I would be able to share a small living space with a Ukrainian-speaking parrot. Added to the other stresses, it could have been enough to cause my breaking point. Eventually, Petrushka and I reached an understanding. He was permitted to enter a room I was already occupying, but only if he would not land on my shoulder. The other rule was he was not allowed to eat off my plate at the dinner table. He did not mind, though, as he had several other plates from which he could choose to dine.

On the Adoption Trail

Our very first morning in Cherkasy started as all other weekday mornings would begin. After breakfast, Natasha and Vladimir #2 picked us up for a full day of bureaucracy battles. We were quite relieved to meet the second Vladimir, as he was much more mature than the first, as was evident in the careful manner in which he drove. We made countless required visits to a growing list of officials to obtain the appropriate stamps and pass out perfume and chocolates. Our first step in Cherkasy was to receive the local authorities' approval to adopt a child from their region.

After we jumped through more bureaucratic hoops, we were granted another meeting at which we were required to explain yet again why we wanted to adopt and also why we thought we could provide a good home for one of their children. The meetings really blurred together. This time our audience was another gold-toothed man, who at first seemed suspicious of us. Once he was convinced our intentions were sincere, he expressed gratitude that Dave and I were helping out one of their children. We received permission to adopt in a record two days. The court date was set for the following Tuesday. To prepare for that, we merely had to fill out more forms, receive more stamps, and pass out more chocolates.

The House of Babies

There was one way to keep motivated through the whole procedure, and that was to fixate our eyes on our goal to bring Katja home with us in order to realize our family vision. Fortunately, I had a tangible tool under my belt—or shall I say in my pocket—to help me do so. Several weeks earlier, we had purchased furniture for Katja's room that required assembly. Either the materials were cheap or else Dave was too strong when he put it together, but somehow one of the dresser knobs split in two. We improvised somehow and instead of throwing these two broken pieces away, I placed them in the pocket of my coat as a literal touchpoint throughout the trip.

Numerous times each day, I would reach for this broken dresser knob as it helped me to visualize Katja's bedroom back home in Montreal. It reminded me that nothing else mattered, which helped to get through even the most trying circumstances. Whenever it felt like we were stuck in a never-ending adminis-trative battle, the familiar feeling of the smooth wood kept our vision to bring Katja into our lives at the top of mind. I refer to this example with my coaching clients when I encourage them to find some tangible means to overcome challenges by reminding them-selves about their vision.

Now that we were in Ukraine, we had an even more powerful reminder of why we were there than broken pieces of wood stashed in my pocket. It was with much excitement that we entered The House of Babies for the very first time. This was the home of our future daughter for the first four years of her life. As we gingerly walked through the muddy and littered yard, we wondered what would await us on the other side of the door. The surroundings of the orphanage were representative of everything we had seen since we landed in Kiev: grey and run-down. The sidewalk heaved and the fence sagged. The only colour in view was the playground equipment provided by Hope Now. Other than that, there was no indication we were not on the grounds of yet another bleak gov-ernment building.

We walked through the big steel doors and once again found ourselves within a dimly lit institution. Natasha led us to Valentina, the director of the orphanage. Valentina graciously accommodated us as we squeezed in as many visits as we could between appointments and document-gathering expeditions. On our first visit, she led us through the long corridors to visit Katja's class of eight children. We walked into the room and immediately felt sixteen eyes staring at us. The worker introduced Katja to her Mama and Papa, to which she responded with a blank look. We were not sure she understood the significance of those two words and, frankly at that stage, neither did we!

From our point of view, we had seen photographs of Katja and had known about her for several months, so it was almost surreal to personally meet her. I compared the whole experience to how I would imagine an arranged marriage might feel. The main difference was that Katja had no concept that she was stuck with us for life.

Eventually, she worked up the courage to approach us, and even be held by us, but she would not make direct eye contact with us on this first day. We were informed that this is typical behaviour for children in her situation. They are not used to having anyone speak with them conversationally and so have not learned how to have focused communication with another person. Some never recover and this trait becomes a symptom of attachment disorder. But with a good dose of love and attention, they can generally become comfortable maintaining eye contact with others. At this stage, Katja still was not too sure about us. She was curious, though.

When Dave would play with the other children, she would watch him intently. As soon as he'd turn around to look at her, she would cast her eyes down. This little game continued for the first couple of meetings. At this point, we just concentrated on helping her feel comfortable with us. We held her and talked to her. We were fully aware that she could not understand a word we said, but we hoped that at least the sounds of our voices would grow on her.

Meanwhile, all the other children played around us. I used the word *played* tentatively, as it was a type of play I had never witnessed before. Everything the children did was structured, quiet, and non-emotional. There were toys in the orphanage but without anyone to model behaviour for them, the children did not know what to do with them. A child would take a toy off the shelf, look at it quietly, walk around the room with it, and then return it. One little boy was playing with an upside-down model car, unsure what to do with it, until Dave flipped it around to demonstrate how to mimic a driving motion. If they were colouring, they would each pick one crayon, scribble without any intention of doing so within the lines of the picture, put back the crayon, pick up another, and start over. There was no indication that they connected their action with the picture drawn on the page.

I do give credit to the House of Babies staff. Considering the scant resources they had available to perform a difficult job, they did their best to treat the children well, albeit with a minimal amount of stimulation. There was also a noticeable lack of physical contact with the children. Part of that could be attributed to a different culture, but for the most part, the staff did not appear to allow themselves to become emotionally attached to the children. As a result, the children were quick to seek attention from outsiders. With a simple touch on the head from us, the children's faces lit up and you could almost see their tears of happiness. By the end of the third day, Dave and I wanted to take the whole group home with us.

The real tragedy is that most children were not eligible for adoption because the parents had not legally given up their parental rights. In some cases, the parents were not able to care for their children at a given point in time, but they hoped to turn their lives around in the future. In many situations, the parents abandoned the children with no intention of ever rearing them, but felt if they kept their parental rights, their children would someday look after them. What they failed to realize is that 90 percent of the boys would end up in jail and a comparative proportion of the girls would end up on the streets.

By the time we visited the orphanage, the Ukrainian law had been recently amended so that if a biological parent did not visit or inquire about their child within a six-month period, they could be adopted out by a Ukrainian family. Then, if the child was not adopted by a Ukrainian family after a period of time, he or she was available for an international adoption. Most of the biological parents knew about the six-month law and so came to visit the orphanage semi-annually, like clockwork, to cling onto their parental rights. We could only hope that future laws would be written to protect the children instead of the parents.

There was one little boy in particular named Sergei who stole our hearts, as well as the hearts of everyone else who had visited the orphanage. Although his parents did not come to visit him, they called Valentina just often enough to retain their parental rights. The fact that his father was in jail and his mother was a drug addict made visitations a little more difficult. We wished the best for his parents, but the reality was that this little boy had no hope for a future due to their actions. We continually reminded ourselves that we could not save everyone on this day. We had to keep our focus on our daughter-to-be. To provide the best possible opportunity for their birth daughter, Katja's biological parents had completed the required paperwork so she was free to be legally adopted by us.

Another pertinent law regarding the orphanage system was that only children under the age of four could be placed in institutions such as The House of Babies. These 'baby' orphanages were much smaller than the large state-run institutions for the older children. It was considerably easier to adopt a child from one of these smaller establishments. Once the children entered the common orphanage at the age of four, they were essentially swallowed up by the system and would typically grow into an adult in that place. I mean adult in the physical sense only. Emotionally and socially, I daresay that the products of the orphanages are far behind their peers.

Although we never saw a state orphanage, we were told they were very bleak compared to The House of Babies. Apparently, these institutions are run more like prisons, simply to handle the logistics of a large number of children within their walls. The ratio of children to caregivers is unmanageably high. Once a child reaches this stage of orphan life, it is very difficult for them to break free from a life of institutionalization. The children are schooled within the grounds, and so must carry the stigma of their past with them throughout life. All of these thoughts raced through my head, as I was fully aware that Katja's fourth birthday was just around the corner—in three short months.

With each visit to The House of Babies, we gradually sensed Katja open up to us. On our fourth day in Cherkasy, we attended her dance class, which was held twice per week. While we could see the workers making an effort to stimulate the children, the activities in the class reinforced the structured environment. The kids mimicked the controlled and robotic actions of the leader. Katja obviously enjoyed her class very much and had a big grin for us the entire time. This was the first moment she seemed to recognize we were there for her. She continually looked for us with her wide smile, as if she needed confirmation that we were still there. Sometimes, she had to lean far back in her chair and crane her neck conspicuously around her classmates to be able to keep us in her line of vision. It was very cute!

One day, we were authorized to whisk Katja away to a city

park. The park consisted of some old, broken-down swings and seesaws, as well as other assorted equipment you might see on old, abandoned school grounds. Luckily there were a few operational swings, along with a small slide, and so we used these to introduce Katja to the world of playgrounds.

As she walked toward the slide, she wrapped her fingers around ours. We helped her up the three short steps and perched her on top of the slide. She had no idea what to do next and so we showed her. This slow, methodical cycle repeated itself five times. In no way could we ascertain whether she was enjoying herself—until we got back to the orphanage, that is. Upon our return, she grinned from ear to ear. This smile continued until we left, which was evidence that she had enjoyed her field trip with us. It was encouraging to imagine what twenty-four hours of normal life would do for her after we witnessed how she reacted to such a common park experience. In case you are wondering, within one week in Canada, Katja ran around parks and slid down slides as if she had experienced them her whole life. We could have never predicted this outcome during our visit to the Cherkasy park that day.

We eagerly looked forward to these visits each day. Sometimes, we even managed to fit in two visits in between schmoozing with the government officials. The time with her passed so quickly it was hard to remember details. She became increasingly accustomed to these strange people she was told to call Mama and Papa. We felt guilty leaving her every day as we wondered how this would influence her image of us in those roles.

Each time we visited the orphanage, Katja was dressed nicely and sporting a big bow literally half the size of her head. After a while, it became apparent there were spies on the grounds who scurried to change her clothes as soon as we were spotted. One time, we managed to surprise the workers and, as soon as we walked in the room, Katja was snatched away and delivered back with new clothes and a big bow in her hair. We tried continuously to communicate with them that, really, *honestly*, the bow was not necessary. On the bright side, she seemed to enjoy the attention.

We were amazed at how well the children behaved. Maybe well-behaved is not the correct term—we were amazed at how *controlled* the children were. For example, at meal or snack time, each child climbed into one of the little chairs like a little soldier. Somehow, they all managed to eat and drink without spilling a single drop or crumb. We marveled at all of those tiny little mouths slurping soup with the aid of what appeared to be a large serving spoon.

Like clockwork, the end of mealtime meant a trip to the potties for everyone. Whether nature called or not, they were forced to sit on their pots for up to thirty minutes, even if they had success right away. When instructed by one of the workers, they all climbed off their pots and headed for the sinks. In synchronized fashion, they rolled up their sleeves and held their hands under the tap as they waited for a worker to turn on the water. After mechanically drying off their hands on their own little towels, they returned to the main room for some scheduled playtime.

The children did not interact with each other in the same way we usually see children play together. On a positive note, we never saw them fight with each other. In retrospect, it would have been refreshing to see at least one member of the group exhibit any dramatic emotion—even anger. The workers spoke to the children, but the little ones rarely spoke back to the adults and almost never to each other.

Little Natasha was an exception to this rule, as she felt inclined to talk for everyone and then some. She was such a little live wire that the thought of her light snuffed out after years of institutional living tugged at our hearts. We would have scooped her up also, but, sadly, she was another child who had been abandoned by parents who would not sign the crucial forms. We had to continually numb ourselves to these tragic situations. We were there for an adoption and we had more work to do. Whenever I needed reminding of why we were there, all I had to do was reach for the dresser knob pieces in my pocket and I was mentally transported back home. Since Katja was part of this vision, there was no choice but to stay focused and keep going.

Chapter Eight

Katja's Adoption (Too Bad We Can't Bring Her Home)

While Katja was warming up to us, so was the local Cherkasy government. I cannot recall every detail of our administrative battles, but we made steady progress. Before we reached any given destination point, Vladimir and Natasha would chatter back and forth in their native tongue to plan our next stop from the front seats while Dave and I were relegated to fulfill the role of backseat tourists. By the time we reached our next stop, Natasha briefed us about our upcoming encounter.

After Vladimir escorted Natasha, Dave, and me out of his jalopy, we would march quietly into another utilitarian government building to meet another nameless official who would interrogate us through Natasha. We would then wait the obligatory half hour or more before the officials would grace our document with their own personal rubber stamp. Then we were free to trundle off to the next bleak establishment. We had complete confidence in Natasha, as we had no idea from one moment to the next what to expect. All I recall for sure is that we continually lightened our load of chocolates and perfume.

We had arrived on Monday and, by Friday, had been granted permission to proceed with Katja's adoption, along with a court date for the following Tuesday. Even more encouraging than winning the bureaucratic battles was the fact that our future daughter continued to respond well to us. At that point, the entire trip was more successful than I had dared hope. On the start of that Friday morning, we anticipated that the upcoming weekend would entail little more than a relaxed tour around Cherkasy and a visit to the market with Vera and her family. That was also the day that our adoption plans fell apart.

Surprisingly, it was not the Ukrainian government that was about to hit us with the next roadblock; it was our own—my old nemesis Immigration Canada, to be exact. We had just returned to Vera's apartment after a successful round of meetings with Ukrainian officials when we received a phone call from the Canadian embassy. I felt extremely confident at that point and so was completely unprepared for what was about to happen.

The woman on the other end wasted no time informing me that, regardless of how our court judgment turned out, our own government would not let us bring our new daughter into our country. This was a setback that was unexpected and very distressing. It seemed ironic that the government who eagerly accepts our hard-earned tax dollars was the one who disappointed us, while our support group back home assumed it would be those big bad foreign Ukrainian government officials who would give us a hard time.

This dimension of our adoption journey is not relevant to the vast majority of adoptions, including other international cases. I share it anyways as some of you may encounter different mountains to climb. Even if you can't imagine making it to the other side, hopefully our story encourages you to take one step at a time towards your goal anyways, and you might surprise yourself on the other side. Personally, I would rather forget this entire turmoil and spare you from the saga, but our Katja story would be incomplete without it.

This particular ordeal really started innocently several weeks before, when Katja was plucked from the orphanage by Natasha for those two rushed doctor visits in Kiev where she sat mute and terrified for twenty minutes. Based on these meetings with Katja, the doctors made quick conclusions that would impact our family greatly. We were not allowed to read the negative feedback in its entirety, but we had general knowledge that the three key issues raised in the report were Katja's lack of responsiveness, which they likened to children with fetal alcohol syndrome, small size, and bilateral cleft lip and palate.

In the few precious hours that we spent with Katja in the orphanage, we were delighted to watch her open up to us like a flower in bloom. Before Katja met us, she was not known to ever try to speak or even smile. After just four days of intermittent displays of love and affection, she ran toward me with her arms outstretched, squawking "Mama, Mama!" Although not an accredited expert on childhood development, I had confidence that after being loved and nurtured for even a short time, Katja would adjust to her new life. I do not want to sound like one of those annoying told-ya-so types, so I will just say that, as it turned out, she didn't just adjust, she *thrived*! HA!

We could not dispute the comments about Katja's size. What shocked me was not that they considered her small. It only required a tape measure and scale to discern that fact. What was disturbing was that this was even considered a potential health issue. Without nutrition, Katja had not grown to her potential height at the age of four. Compared to her peers in the orphanage, she was of average size. I could not fathom that a child raised in an orphanage would have anything but delayed development. At least it cleared up a mystery for me. I had always wondered why Canadians were relatively tall compared to citizens of some other countries. Until this point, I thought it had something to do with genetics or a good diet. Now I knew the truth. Apparently, some short people were simply blocked from immigrating.

The other fact that could not be contested in the report was that Katja was born with a cleft lip and palate, though we disagreed with our government's reaction to this very treatable condition. Canada is lauded worldwide for its wonderful social safety net for such services as medical coverage for all citizens. Throughout our careers in Canada, Dave and I have paid and continue to pay dearly in the form of taxes to do our part to keep our various supports fully functioning. We were happy, though, to have this safety net in case we ever had to rely on it for our own family. Imagine our disappointment to discover the services we paid for were not available to our own family.

To make a political statement was not on our list of priorities. Our first concern was to release Katja from the orphanage and bring her home, so we were prepared to circumvent the regular procedures. No matter our entitlement to the medical system we supported, we offered to relinquish any rights Katja would have to medical care in Canada. Anything was better than leaving her in the orphanage for an indeterminate amount of time.

We made another call to Vic Jackopson in England. Immediately he made a very generous proposal. Vic offered the resources of Hope Now to pay for all future medical care for Katja, if the Canadian government would just let her into her adoptive country. He sent us such a confirmation and we immediately forwarded the document on to our officials, but it did not matter. There was no way they would let us enter the country with our daughter.

And so we had to tell our Ukrainian hosts and helpers that our daughter could not accompany us to Canada. There we were, guests in a country of considerable poverty, and we had to explain that Canada refused to let our daughter into the country lest she require speech therapy and surgeries. We hid our maple leaves inside our coats that day.

The workers at the Canadian embassy in Kiev seemed genuinely sorry for our predicament. They could only do their job and, in the most humane way possible, tried to justify such unjustifiable bureaucracy. But their hands were tied. Therefore, we knew prior to our official adoption court date that we would likely be forced to leave the country without Katja.

Needless to say, this was very discouraging and frustrating and at first Dave and I were left with a sense of defeat. After we had endured (and still had not won) the long battles to get pregnant, then made the decision to adopt after careful consideration, which led to eight months of bureaucratic battles and corre$ponding payment$ to various parties, we could not believe we were facing yet another battle. This initial sense of defeat rapidly changed to preparations to take up bureaucratic arms with our government. Even while in Ukraine, we received an overwhelming response from family and friends who were kept abreast of our progress. There was never a doubt that we would go through with our court date. Fortunately, I had a broken dresser knob in my pocket that continually reminded me we just had to take one step at a time as each one moved us closer to realizing our vision.

Our Day in Court

So we entered the courtroom with mixed feelings. The court experience itself was uneventful. Across from us sat a very stern-faced female judge who interrogated us through our ever-loyal interpreter, Natasha. The judge managed to sustain a very serious expression on her face the entire time we stood in her courtroom. It was a look of boredom, with a bit of irritation and a dash of disdain thrown in. She asked questions in a monotone manner and it seemed to pain her to have to speak in our general direction. Not once did she bother to look at us. If she had any positive thoughts toward us, her mind had certainly not informed her face.

Most of the initial queries were straightforward and thus very easy to answer. In fact, I thought we got away a little too easily when the only information she requested was our name and address. The situation intensified a bit when she asked us to rise individually and give a little impromptu speech about why we wanted to adopt one of their children. Two disturbing thoughts ran through my head. First, why was she so disinterested in what we had to say? Furthermore, while I knew what I would say, I did not know if Dave was as mentally prepared for this critical question.

Determined to persevere through the interview, I summarized our entire family expansion efforts. In response, our personality-challenged judge asked through Natasha if we were just adopting a child as a rebound effect, as if our miscarriage was comparable to a bad break-up. While I adamantly stated this was not the case, that familiar thought suddenly struck me that she could probably speak fluent English and that the need for an interpreter was staged as a ploy to fluster us. I still needed to answer the question. By this stage, it was clear in my mind why we were proceeding with this adoption and so I was able to respond appropriately.

I recommend to others heading to adoption court to have their explanation firmly implanted in their minds. By the time you are through your home study, you will likely have a clear answer.

After a trying half hour in court, our sourpuss judge authorized our adoption. And so, just like that, we became the official legal parents of Katja. There were just a few more signatures to obtain, after which the judge surprisingly expressed to Natasha that she really liked us. Boy, I shudder to think how she would treat someone she did not like. The rest of the day passed quickly as we arranged to have Katja's new birth certificate prepared, which was the first document that would officially list us as the parents.

Optimistic that she would someday be able to travel with us, we also set out to obtain her passport. For the last time, we waited for hours in a long corridor listening to the continual hum of heavy doors opening and slamming shut. Ten days prior, this noise had been disconcerting, but now it was comforting as we knew one of the slams would eventually lead us to our document.

By the end of the day, we were in more of a celebratory mood than ever, regardless of the battle that lay ahead. We convinced Vladimir to pull over to the side of the road. In the backseat of his run-down Lada, on some side street in the middle of Cherkasy, Ukraine, Dave and I toasted each other with one of the remaining bottles of wine in our gift bag as we celebrated the new addition to our family.

We tried relentlessly throughout our last two days in Ukraine to convince Immigration Canada to allow us to come home with our daughter. By this point, they had received the written proof that Hope Now was committed to pay for any surgeries that remained, as well as to help with future expenses. Although the premise behind the refusal of Katja's immigration was medical costs, their elimination from the equation did not make a difference.

In the end, we just had to face the harsh reality that we would have to return home without our daughter and fight this battle on our home field. Our last visit with Katja was very painful. We showered her with extra hugs and kisses and hoped the staff would be able to adequately explain that Mama and Papa would be back soon. It broke my heart to leave her, as she had dared to let her guard down with us and began to give and receive affection freely.

While we said goodbye to Katja, the words of my contact at the Canadian embassy resonated in my head. According to her, we would have to wait a minimum of six months before getting the proper papers to bring Katja home. Somehow, we were expected to accept this as a viable solution while we left our daughter in the orphanage to wonder where her parents had gone. There was no way that anybody could prevent us from realizing our vision at this point.

I had packed toys and food for Katja's trip home, but none of that was needed. We had prepared ourselves for a hectic return trip but instead it was quiet. However, it was anything but relaxed. I knew our mission would begin as soon as we reached Montreal. The operation had changed from the Adopt Katja Project to the Bring Katja Home Campaign.

Chapter Nine

The Bring Katja Home Campaign

We returned to Montreal ready to battle the Canadian government. We were prepared to plead with various political parties, media personalities, and almost anyone who would listen, until we could find somebody to help us. I had never planned to be a political activist, but I was about to get a crash course. I just could not accept that it would be several months, if not years, before we could be together as a family.

We were told by politicians and bureaucrats at several different levels that:

- there was nothing they could do;

- we were not the first to feel this way; and

- (my personal favourite) our request was not normal procedure.

Many memories of frustration flooded back as I retraced my steps to gather documents much like I had begun to do nine months previously. For example, I tried calling one government department for assistance and, because my call was transferred to no less than five different people, I was forced to explain our situation five times, alternating in French and English. After the fifth conversation, I was transferred again, but this time to the original listener. In exasperation I hung up and never did call back! I knew quitting was not an option, but there were definitely times when I could have justified it, and this was one of them.

Not only was the process exasperating, but the entire immigration system worked against us. Canada allows a relatively large number of immigrants through its borders. Around the time we adopted Katja, over 200,000 immigrants were allowed into Canada each year. If an immigrant was sponsored by a family member, the process would take six months to a year to complete. As our daughter was born in another country, she was treated in the same way as any other family-sponsored immigrant.

The system is designed to screen out anyone who might excessively use any part of the social safety net. Thus, immigration hinges on the medical exam that Katja had supposedly failed. Notwithstanding the fact that we had anecdotal proof that disagreed with the doctors' conclusions, Katja was our daughter and therefore our dependent. She belonged with us.

We were granted a deadline of ten weeks to provide any further medical information to correct the misdiagnosis. Otherwise, the opinion would remain as a big ugly stain on Katja's record. If we could not get the medical opinion changed, at some point Katja would be able to enter Canada with a special Minister's Permit. We were reassured that Katja would probably end up with us, but it would be a matter of at least six months. I started to respect the

Ukrainian methods that required comprehensive documentation before any type of decision could be made.

I tried to poke holes through Katja's medical analysis. First, we sent reconfirmation that Katja would not in any way use the Canadian medical system to try and take this completely out of the judgment. We even made arrangements for her surgeries to occur in Oxford, England. Unfortunately, there was no way to strike the surgery requirement from her record.

As for Katja's small stature, I did not really want to dignify such a useless comment with a response, but I was willing to do whatever it took. I provided medical opinions from doctors who stated that any child with Katja's background would be smaller than the average North American scales would dictate. This seemed logical to me.

I felt the most significant point the officials would focus on was the potential for Katja to need special education. I was able to obtain several reports from medical personnel who had met Katja throughout her first four years that confirmed they witnessed a clever girl who was merely under-stimulated. I forwarded these reports to Immigration Canada in the hopes that a human at the other end would process the information instead of a machine with an accept or reject stamp.

Who is Immigration, Anyway?

Around every corner, I would be told that the matter at hand was for Immigration. Or I was reassured by someone that they would call Immigration right away. I was not convinced that real, live people were part of this thing called Immigration. It sounded like an inanimate machine that was fed information and would spit out an answer. Pull the string and Immigration says, "Sorry, there is nothing we can do." Pull it again and the message is, "No matter what, your forms will take months to complete." There are only a handful of allowable responses and the others are equally annoying to someone on an immigration mission.

We were told that, once the second opinion was given, Immigration would be able to start gathering more documents to start initiating the process to get the procedure in place. It was very convoluted, but the message was clear that if we followed the normal rules and procedures, there was no way this problem could be solved quickly. I was a bit worried when I was asked to consider going to Ukraine for several months with Katja while the documents got sorted out. I did not like the implication that this would be such a drawn-out procedure.

Battle fatigue started to wear me down. I was sure I irritated all government bodies with whom I had contact. I even irritated myself! Perhaps I subconsciously hoped they would all get so fed up with my constant barrage of phone calls and emails that they would miraculously grant our daughter the appropriate papers to come live with her parents.

Meanwhile, the media continually fed us stories about how some citizens of Canada abused the social systems. Especially rampant were stories about people who were granted visitors' visas to the United States and then literally walked over the border to be granted asylum in Canada. Canada was so generous at that time that every person who asked for asylum was granted it. Why did we not think of that option? Walking over the border illegally would have been much quicker and easier than filling out the forms and jumping through the required hoops to get her into the country through the proper channels.

To keep the vision alive through this ordeal, I clung to my memories of Katja, with the aid of the pictures we were with her. Even though we were back home, I kept the dresser knob in my coat pocket for a continual reminder of the vision. Now that we were half a world apart, many of our bureaucratic Ukrainian experiences seemed surreal. Our time with Katja was different and those memories were vivid. This made the delays even more frustrating. We worried about what she would think of us. Would she be mad at us? Or, worse, would she forget about us? We had made so much progress with her that we did not want to lose the momentum. By thinking and talking about her, I continued to feel connected.

The misdiagnosis that led to our predicament was not the main issue to conquer as that was a done deal. At the root was that Katja was being treated the same as if we were sponsoring an adult family member to come to Canada. It did not matter that the immigrant in question was a little girl who would not be in a position to abuse the system. It did not matter that she would be fully dependent on Dave and myself. It did not matter that she was stuck in an orphanage in the middle of Ukraine while we had to follow the cumbersome procedures. We were expected to be comforted by the fact that Katja's immigration would be rushed as are all family cases, and that the six months it might take was much better than the usual three years to complete an immigration. The officials with whom I spoke did not seem to understand the ramifications of leaving Katja in the orphanage for an additional six months of this formative period of her life.

The absurdity of the immigration procedure was summed up on the four-page application for permanent residency that Katja was required to fill out. Luckily, as her mother, I was able to complete it for her. At this point, I counted my blessings that she did not need to first learn English, fill in the form herself, and then submit it. This grossly irrelevant form asked for such information of Katja as:

- *Her marital status, date and place of marriage, and if she had been married more than once.* Although there was one little boy in the orphanage she played with, we took the initiative to assume she was single.

- *Personal details of all her dependents.* This was a little frightening—what if our new four-year-old daughter was supporting somebody we didn't know about. Would we be responsible for her dependents, also?

- *Her ability to speak, read, and write in English and French.* This requirement is too ridiculous for me to comment.

- *Education history.* Ditto to the above.

- *Work history for the past ten years.* All we observed was block-building and colouring.

- *Her list of assets.* Now we are getting to the good stuff!

- *Her list of debts or legal obligations.* Uh oh, we had never thought of this before.

- *Her address over the past ten years.* Orphanage. Check.

- *Organizations to which she has belonged since her eighteenth birthday.* She had not yet reached her fourth.

- Finally, a variety of questions asking if she had ever applied for and/or been denied immigration to anywhere, including Canada.

Although I can laugh now at the absurdity of the questions I was required to answer, I was perplexed at the time as to what to write down on the form, as every question required a response in order for our application to even be considered. Many of the very kind and patient individuals I spoke to along the way agreed that the

THE POCKET ADOPTION COACH

system was not fair and said the laws were under review. It would have been easier if we could have blamed one person instead of an entire system of immigration laws within a country. The latter is much more difficult to beat. I was not sure how we would ever break through the red and white tape of the Canadian government.

Turning Point

The most positive aspect of this whole experience was the overwhelming support we received from friends and family. My brother was working as a journalist, and we drew upon his political knowledge as he led the Bring Katja Home Campaign. He was more familiar with the inner workings of both the government and the media. Together, we made countless phone calls and sent numerous messages to politicians, opposition parties, and media personalities. Others in our support group sent messages to the immigration department. While coordinating this effort, I prayed that the politicians in Ottawa would surrender, if only to never have to hear from us again. We were definitely the squeaky wheel.

Before this series of events, I had zero experience as a politically active citizen. I certainly did my civic duty at the polls and tried to keep abreast of major events in the world, but beyond that I had never taken a personal interest in what our elected politicians did with their time and my money. Boy, did that change overnight! If I came across a news story on television, radio, or newsprint about our leaders' activities, I was comforted knowing that at least somebody was at work. I just hoped that one of them had read our letters earlier that day.

Several issues heightened our levels of exasperation. The first was the passing of an anniversary. While not an event to be celebrated, I recognized at this time that exactly one year had passed

~ 143 ~

since the miscarriage. Through this entire chaos, we still dared to hope that we would get pregnant in order to supply a little brother or sister for Katja. That whole infertility nuisance compounded the emotional turmoil around bringing Katja home.

As well, we seriously needed a plumber to fix the steady leak from our bank account. This extra phase had resulted in numerous additional lengthy three-dollar-per-minute phone calls to Ukraine, not to mention an extra trip overseas. This was more than we bargained for financially at this point. We knew that having children in the home would result in a steady outflow of cash. At least then our money would be well-spent on caring for our children's needs and not wasted on these unnecessary expenses caused by a broken bureaucratic system.

I finally reached my breaking point. I had hoped it would come in the privacy of our home, but that was not meant to be. We had come to a critical point in our plans, and I was caught in a vicious circle I could not break.

We were trying to bring Katja into Canada through the back door by arranging for a surgery prior to her arrival. We wanted to prove to the Canadian officials that this would be done without the aid of the Canadian tax-based system. We had a plan. Fitting with the entire theme, it was problematic, but it could work. Someone would fly with Katja from Ukraine to England, for which both would need a travel visa, to come for the surgery. This plan would not be easy as it required:

- obtaining two visitor visas for Katja and her travel companion;
- arranging accommodations in England;
- scheduling a surgery; and

- planning my own travel plans to meet Katja and her travel companion in the UK.

It was quite complicated, but all of the details were pulled together within a few days.

The only step left was to obtain the visa for Katja and her guardian to enter England. Understandably, for a visitor visa, the British government required an end date. We had to supply a date that we could take Katja out of the country. We could not send her back to the orphanage after such a traumatic event and after spending an extended period with me in England. All we had to do was find a country that would let us in. As accommodating as the English were, they would not let Katja stay there indefinitely with a visitor visa. So, where would she go? I pictured that we would sit in an airplane and circle the world until a country would be so kind as to let us enter its borders.

I tried to explain our predicament to a sweet but do-it-by-the-book employee of our local Member of Parliament in the west island of Montreal. We had already spoken several times and as she had so eloquently relayed to me in a prior conversation, "You know, Michele, everyone thinks their case is the most important." I have always been annoyed when people use my name in a condescending tone to try to get a point across that they think is trivial. I had already experienced this tone with this individual, so I braced myself during this visit. I explained that we could not get Katja into Canada until she had her surgery, but she could not have her surgery until we had permission to bring her to Canada afterward.

I pleaded for a solution when I received the disheartening response that I expected. While it was unfortunate our daughter was stuck in the orphanage without access to the medical attention she needed, the process had to be followed. I could feel my eyes stinging and the lump in my throat expanding. This was our last chance to reverse the medical report, and she was not budging one inch. After this, Katja's file would be relegated to the slow track and we would not see her again for months. At this point there was not even a glimmer of hope that anything could be done.

I looked down and tried to keep the door of the dam shut tightly. Despite my best efforts, it burst and I lost my control right there. The big ugly cry. All of my frustrations were let out in front of this hapless worker. It was not pretty. I mopped up my tears and went home, not expecting any further results for several more weeks. Even after all we had experienced, this was the lowest point of all.

Imagine my shock when our Member of Parliament called me the very next day! I believe that his competent, yet unimaginative employee did not ever want to see me again. She relayed the details about my visit and so he decided to champion our cause. He had read several letters written by our group of personal lobbyists and immediately agreed to take our case to the Minister of immigration in Ottawa for some quick action. Finally, somebody listened!

Two days later, he called again to inform us that he had conducted an informal meeting with the Minister in Ottawa about our case and had been able to get a Minister's Permit granted on the spot. This would not give Katja a status of permanent resident; that battle would still have to be fought. The only issue was that since Katja could only have a Ukrainian passport, we could not take her across the Canadian border without a special visa. This was a small price to pay to have our daughter live with us full-time. We were told that the Minister's Permit would have to be renewed each year (for a fee, of course) for five years, at which time Katja would be granted automatic citizenship. Compared to what we had already experienced, this was a minor inconvenience.

And so, I found myself planning another overseas trip for two with a return flight for three. All of the international adoption literature warns adoptive parents to be ready to travel with little to no advance warning. I was sure that would not pertain to us, as I had planned everything so carefully. I forgot to plan for the events out of my control! The logistics of the trip were tricky and so our situation changed from a political to a practical problem. We were not quite out of the woods yet.

Entering a former Communist country presented unique challenges. Letters of invitation were required in order to receive the visa needed to cross in and out of the border. The visas we had in our passports were due to expire on April 15, and it was already the end of March. If we were not able to pick up Katja and leave Ukraine before April 15, we would have to apply for, and then wait for, new visas. This process was in itself lengthy and quite expensive. We were warned that it would take several days before we would obtain the Minister's Permit. We really crossed our fingers that the permit would come quickly to avoid the visa mess. In anticipation that the logistics would miraculously work out, I arranged for the services of a driver and our interpreter Natasha, as well as our overnight accommodations for when we eventually arrived in Ukraine—at a date to be determined.

Once again in our adoption story, we experienced what others had said was impossible. We received the Minister's Permit in record time. Somehow, all the paperwork and red tape were completed within one day. The struggles overcome and battles fought up to that point to bring Katja home were temporarily forgotten, as we were so close to having her with us. All we really wanted to do was to return to Ukraine, scoop Katja up, and bring her home.

Chapter Ten

The Pick-Up

O ur first trip to Ukraine had turned out to be false labour. This time, we were booked for a caesarean section and just had to follow the tight schedule. No amount of previous travel experience could have prepared us for the whirlwind trip we planned. Our itinerary was shocking, even for the airline agents. We left Montreal on the afternoon of Saturday, April 4, to arrive in Zurich on April 5, just in time to hang around the airport half the day before flying out to Kiev. We would then turn around on April 6, overnight in Zurich, and return to Montreal on Tuesday, April 7. This provided a one-week buffer before our visas expired.

After we reached Zurich, we thought the rest of the trip was smooth sailing. One more rough patch was ahead of us. Again, it was an emotional breakdown on my part that saved the day! Flying standby is never an easy task, especially if the arrival at the other end of the journey is extremely important. Dave's job was affiliated with the airlines and so we were able to purchase standby tickets at a significantly discounted fare. Contrary to my better judgment, we used standby tickets for this crucial flight. We had never experienced a problem, and so decided to take our chances.

All went well from Montreal to Zurich. The next leg of our journey was Zurich to Kiev. We were so close to the finish line, only to be informed there was no room for us on the plane. The problem was not that all seats were taken, it was that the weight on the plane was too much to accept standby passengers like us. Our cheap fares did not cover the extra fuel required to lift us off to Kiev. Our flight was to leave Zurich at noon, and by 11:55 a.m., we still did not know if we would get on it. I frantically called Natasha every ten minutes as she and the driver needed to leave for the airport to pick us up. It was a two-hour drive, which was approximately the length of time it would take for us to fly in from Switzerland.

Throughout the whole adoption process, there were a number of times when I involuntarily leveraged the fact that our project carried a heavy emotional price tag. This was one of those times that my emotions took over and may have won us a sympathy vote. In earnest, I explained to the ticketing agent that our tiny little adopted daughter was waiting for us at the other end. After months of distress, our family would finally be complete, as long as we could board this plane. I got the impression from the rather stern boarding airline agent that my message did not compel her to change direction.

Just a few minutes before take-off, all full-fare passengers were called to board the plane. We watched them, one by one and two by two, board the ark, wondering if there would be space for us once they had all boarded. I had never before paid any attention to how much luggage my fellow passengers carried on an airplane, but this time I was very cognizant that everyone seemed to be hauling hefty bags and boxes. The situation looked pretty grim.

One minute before the plane was scheduled to leave, Dave and I were called to the desk. Various scenarios played in my head as I was bracing myself for the news. The significance of a delay was compounded by the fact that connections throughout the week were very tight. Therefore, to postpone our trip by just one day would have meant postponing it by several days, which would put us dangerously close to the expiration date on our Ukrainian visa.

I imagine the expression on my face was one of terror, panic, desperation, and sadness all rolled into one ball of stress. I don't recall my exact behaviour, but faintly recall Dave trying to dis-associate himself from me at that moment! The details are a bit fuzzy as the situation intensified. Tears may have been involved. All that mattered was that somehow the airline officials changed their minds. I suspect they just wanted me out of their airport. I didn't blame them, but most importantly, they allowed us on the airplane just minutes before takeoff.

From that point forward, I am pleased to report that all of our plans went off without a hitch. Natasha met us at the airport with Vladimir #3. I figured out by this point that not only must all drivers be named Vladimir, but none of them could speak English. That way, we were required to pay for the services of both a driver and a translator at all times. This system is further perpetuated by the fact that none of the translators can drive.

There were no meetings with government officials. We had no further papers to file. All we had to do that day was ride down to Cherkasy with Natasha and Vladimir and have a quick visit with Katja before turning in for the evening at Vera's apartment.

This trip was much more pleasant than our first one. It was daylight, there was no fog, and our third Vladimir was a good and cautious driver. I still vowed that the next time, we would be more selective about the country from which we adopted. I mused that perhaps Cancun or the Cayman Islands would be good options.

We Meet Again!

On Sunday, April 5, we would at last be reunited with our daughter. Our last goodbyes to her had occurred on March 4—just over one month had passed. Throughout that month, the staff at The House of Babies had ensured that Katja remembered her parents—these people who swept into her routine life, gave her love and attention for ten days, and then magically disappeared. This would not exactly give us the title of model parents by any standards.

I was nervous as we neared the orphanage, as I was not sure what Katja's reaction would be. I knew that children are forgiving, but this would be especially difficult for her to comprehend. Several days before our second arrival, Natasha had asked Katja if she remembered her mother and father and if she was waiting for them to come back to her. Miraculously, Katja replied, "da" on both counts. In the last month, I had been so wrapped up in fighting for Katja's immigration papers that it served as a distraction to the real issue, which was how she coped with this very confusing situation. It was safer not to think about it. Soon, we would find out how this last month had affected Katja through her reaction to us.

We arrived at the orphanage early that evening. This would be a brief stop, as the children were getting ready for bed. We tentatively intruded in her room, as we awaited her greeting. Katja's big blue eyes peeked at us around the corner and seemed to beg the question, "It is nice of you to drop by, but what are you doing here?" She came to us, but more slowly than on our last goodbye visit one month before. She did not run with her arms outstretched. She seemed confused. Not unhappy, just confused. We stayed for a few hugs and then, for the last time, deserted our daughter for the night.

We were happy to have the opportunity to see our friend Vera and her family again. So much had happened and changed since we'd left them that it seemed like much longer than the month it was. After a quick visit and a short, restless sleep, we prepared to return to the orphanage the following morning armed with clothes, toys, and food for our daughter.

We Are Parents!

We have heard numerous celebrities muse about how ironic it was that they had been labelled an overnight success when they had lived anonymously in their car for years before anyone had heard of them. That is how I suddenly felt about becoming parents overnight. Even though months and years of preparation had brought us to this point, suddenly we were only moments away from our lives being radically altered by a two-foot-nine-inch, twenty-five-pound little girl.

It is true that our lives changed dramatically overnight. That is just the way parenthood is. One day you are childless and the next day you are a parent. Wham! Suddenly I found myself second-guessing my decisions in this new and unfamiliar territory. For example, when I packed clothes for Katja, I'd struggled to decide what size to bring. Sometimes the mind plays tricks. In this case, Katja grew in my mind to be quite a bit bigger than she was. I was concerned about bringing clothes that would be too small for her, so I went up a size or two. That turned out to be a mistake as she was swimming in the outfits I picked for her homecoming trip. I worried the orphanage workers would not let Katja go with such an incompetent mother. Katja was just so happy to be in her new, ill-fitting clothes that it really did not matter.

Also, on our first trip I had not paid much attention to the fact that none of the Vladimirs' cars had seat belts in the backseat. This was a common occurrence, as seat-belt usage was not a requirement. I felt uneasy about escorting Katja on a two-hour car ride without a seat belt. In North America, such behaviour would be illegal, and possibly borderline abuse. I found this to be such a paradox, as the children were over-protected at the orphanage in so many ways, while seat belts were optional if and when they ever left the grounds.

We all made it to the airport in one piece and then had to say goodbye to Natasha. She had become such an integral part of our lives during an intense time and so it was hard to imagine that we would not be in regular contact. Otherwise, it was a very happy day for all as we were finally boarding a plane with Katja and heading for home together. (We didn't know it at the time, but we would meet up with Natasha one more time in Canada to celebrate Katja's twelfth birthday but that is another story.)

Throughout the whole trip, the only time Katja exhibited nervousness was while in the presence of immigration officials at the Zurich airport. We were asked to wait in an institutional-looking room while they checked our papers. We were directed by a man in a uniform. Immediately, Katja stiffened and started to cry. She probably thought we were leaving her there. So far, as parents, we did not have a great track record in her eyes. As soon as we were released from the office, she was once again a happy traveller.

When we arrived at the hotel in Zurich, Dave and I were comforted by much familiarity around us. After all, we had lived in the country for over two years. However, in some ways, we felt like strangers in our own lives.

Katja seemed unfazed as she sat very still with us at the restaurant. People had reassured us that children can adapt to new situations much more easily than adults, but I would have never imagined she could have done so well given all the new circumstances facing her. She could not even get any comfort from our reassurances, as she could not understand a word we said. That was unfortunate as things were about to get unexpectedly stressful very quickly.

As any typical parents do, we ran a bath for Katja at night. As soon as the water came out of the spout, Katja began to belt out blood-curdling screams. We had no idea that this unassuming little girl who had barely said boo her first four years could reach such a decibel level. We were a little self-conscious as we knew everyone on the floor in the hotel, as well as the floor above and below, must have wondered what we were doing to torture this poor child. I tried my best to soothe Katja, but something terrified her. Somehow, we would have to work through this issue when we got home, but for now, we tucked her into the hotel bed, and she slept soundly the entire night.

Other than this incident, Katja had a relatively easy trip home, which was a big relief. Dave and I would not have had a clue what to do had she been completely traumatized leaving her familiar surroundings with these quasi-stranger-parental shadow figures. After all of the work and energy to bring Katja home, all I could think was that maybe the officials had all made a big mistake. What did we know about parenting? How could they let us take a child away? But they had, and so we started the parenting cycle of doing our best and learning on the job. Our education would begin as soon as we boarded our flights for home.

I did not know what Katja would eat, so I brought jars of baby food. Even though she was almost four years old, she was underdeveloped and would not have had exposure to many foods. I thought she might feel queasy on the flights home, so I thought baby food would be the safest bet. This was my first personal experience with maternal instinct, and I was right. Too bad we didn't listen to it.

On the two plane rides home—from Kiev to Zurich on the first day, and then Zurich to Montreal the following day—Katja was offered a special children's meal of chicken nuggets and french fries. Her eyes widened at the quantity of the food and she loved the taste immediately. It was so adorable and heartwarming to watch her gobble down this novel food. We giggled as she chomped down every bite. We were so happy to see her with a good appetite, so we also shared our meals with Katja. All seemed to go well, until our first day at home. We paid for our lack of restraint with a little girl in extreme pain. Katja had severe digestion difficulties. With the help of a suppository, we learned that it was important to gradually introduce her to new foods.

Home Sweet Home

Upon arriving in Montreal, we were ready to begin our new daily life as a family. I will never forget the look on Katja's face when she walked through the door of her new house. The best word I can use to describe it is lost. For twenty minutes, she just stood in her new bedroom and stared at me. A sudden wave of guilt washed over me as I wondered what we had done to this poor child. Just the previous morning, she had woken up in surroundings she had known her whole life and now she suddenly had nothing familiar around her. Except, of course, for these two people who repeatedly popped in and out of her life.

After this twenty-minute stare-down, Katja started to open up to her surroundings. She realized that the toys were hers and the clothes in the closet were hers and that these parents were hers. Shortly thereafter, she ran around the house as if she had lived there for her first four years of life.

One incident did occur in these first moments that was troubling. A dear friend had left a big rag doll to greet Katja. When I introduced Katja to her new baby, the first action Katja took was to spank the doll very hard, set it firmly on the ground, and shake her finger at it. For a flashing moment, I worried that Katja had suffered physical abuse at the orphanage. I did not really believe it could be true, as we had met the staff at The House of Babies. While the children were not stimulated to the extent that we would consider normal, we did not witness any sign that they had been excessively physically disciplined in such a manner.

Katja's introduction to her doll is an event we can never fully understand. What I do know is that, by the end of that first day, Katja exhibited great love and care for all of her dolls. She spent hours feeding, dressing, bathing, and potty-training them. To this day, the biggest impression Katja makes on other people is how concerned she is for others, especially young children. Had I been able to see into the future while I watched Katja hit her doll, I would not have been alarmed. But I did not have a crystal ball and so I had a few anxious moments wondering what lay ahead.

Then we still had to deal with the bath issue. Each night, as we neared bath-time, I dreaded Katja's reaction. And, each night, we were greeted with her shrieks of terror at the mere sight of water coming from the taps and into the bathtub. I resorted to quick sponge baths and not even that was acceptable for her. Since bathing was not optional, we needed to get Katja accustomed to the idea. My mother came to the rescue with an idea. Given Katja's love of dolls, what if we bathed her dolls as part of playtime? It worked like a charm. We drew a big bathtub full of warm water and bubbles and pretended to bathe her dolls. The next day, she was delighted to join them. Katja happily played in the bathtub for long periods every night thereafter.

Ironically, Katja quickly earned her nickname of "The Fish" due to her love of water. She not only grew to love baths, but two favourite pastimes became running through the sprinkler and swimming. The first time Katja took swimming lessons, other children were nervous and had to be coaxed into the pool. Not our Katja, though. She was the first to jump in, submerge her head, and start swimming. The other parents all commented on how very comfortable our daughter, The Fish, was in the water. Little did they know the irony of their observation.

I wish I knew why Katja had reacted so violently to her bath. Obviously, the children in the orphanage were cleaned by some method, so it was not the first time she would have seen water and soap. I have been told that the children may have just been sprayed down to be cleaned and so a bathtub was likely a new experience for her. That would explain her reluctance to enter it, but it fails to explain why just being wiped with a wet cloth was so traumatic. Parents of children adopted at an older age must learn to let go of the need to have such answers. This was not a comfortable feeling for me. However, Katja was ready to move on and so I had to leave it behind to keep up with her.

During those first few weeks, Katja would go through spurts of running from corner to corner of the house in a frenzied state to see everything she could within a small period. Then she would calm right down to prepare for another round of enthusiastic exploration. Dave and I enjoyed some built-in entertainment as we sat back and observed her adaptation process. We did not accomplish much else in those first few weeks.

Katja assimilated so well that I often forgot she could not understand a word of English. I spoke to her in a language foreign to her ear, but she was able to pick up cues and respond appropriately. I remember the first word I heard her say other than Mama and Papa. I was cleaning the bathroom when suddenly these two little arms shot straight toward me and I clearly heard the word "up." Katja had made her first verbal request! So, I did what any proud mother would—I dropped what I was doing and picked her up. Luckily, Katja was able to learn English much more quickly than Dave and I learned Russian.

Attachment

Before we brought Katja home, my concern was not that we could not attach to our new daughter. We knew that we already had. We were more concerned about how she would react to us, as well as others around her.

At the beginning of this book, I shared some of the less positive reactions we heard when we announced our decision to adopt an older child. We heard stories about such difficult transitions that the adoptive parents were ready to send their new child back to the orphanage. Within one week, nobody could have guessed she had recently been plucked from a Ukrainian orphanage and transported into her life. Through the weeks that followed, we watched her become a spirited and charismatic little girl who won over people's hearts. Within two days, Katja learned how to give and receive kisses and, another two days later, she became the best hugger.

She also gained confidence that we would always be there for her. She had no doubt that we were her Mama and Papa. When she met someone new, Katja would observe them for a period of time. Once she was sure they were safe, she would venture forth and open up to others, as well. This discernment comforted me as Katja showed an ability to form real and lasting relationships.

Playing Techniques

Due to the generosity of Hope Now, The House of Babies had some toys for the children. But as we observed in the orphanage, they did not know what to do with them. This was not surprising given that no parents or other role models played alongside them to demonstrate. I wondered how Katja would learn how to play in a way that our society would deem appropriate for her chronological age.

She quickly latched onto her favourite toys, which consisted primarily of dolls, a kitchen play set, and anything else she needed to nurture her plastic babies. We also introduced her to toys and games designed for children aged zero to three, as she needed to gain skills to progress to toys meant for her age group. Without experiencing this with Katja firsthand, I would not have realized how crucial play time is for a child's development. It sounds almost as complicated as a college curriculum. You cannot graduate to the cardboard puzzles until you have mastered the wooden ones. The skills required to play with Lego are to be learned through playing with large building blocks.

For most children, this progression is gradual and so parents may not remark on the hour during which a child suddenly becomes bored with a particular toy and ready to move onto the next level. In Katja's case, she fast forwarded through these developmental stages within weeks. She passed through each phase she'd missed before leaping into the next round of learning. Fortunately for our budget, we were receiving a constant supply of toys from family and friends, and so did not have to privately fund this accelerated learning curve.

Eating Habits

Katja loved to eat any food we presented to her including prunes, which came in handy! And eat and eat. Initially, her preoccupation with food led to distress when a meal was over. Her body cried out for more. Although Katja was almost four, she was smaller than an average North American two-year-old. We do not know the entire menu plan at the orphanage. Most of what we saw the children eat was starch, as that was the least expensive way to ward off hunger. I understand that a diet of protein and vitamins was not a priority, and it showed.

Not only was Katja small, but she also had a distended stomach. At first, we worried that we were overfeeding our daughter when we took note of her bloated belly. As I watched her stomach diminish as she ate more food, I realized how malnourished she had been. During Katja's first two months with us, she gained two inches and we watched her body morph into that of a healthy child.

We learned from our suppository experience that it was up to us, the parents, to set limits on what Katja could tolerate. She did not like the limits, though. Gradually, Katja relaxed at mealtime as she came to trust that there would be another meal to follow the current one. I was quite surprised when she voluntarily pushed her plate away for the first time. She even had the audacity to discover there were some foods she did not like. This was a far cry from the first days, when she would have eaten paper if we had fed it to her. Eventually, she even rejected the prunes.

In parallel to reality, much of Katja's playtime was focused on meals. She pretended to make food on her stove. She mixed pretend food in her plastic bowls. She dressed her dolls in bibs so they were ready to eat at a moment's notice. She then fed her dolls and seemed determined that they too would never lack food.

Katja was also one of the neatest eaters I had ever met. She was so careful not to spill her food or drink on the table. Then one day, as children do, she knocked over her cup and the milk inside poured onto the table and floor. We will never know for certain how the workers would have reacted to such an accident at the orphanage, but her terrified look and anguished cries suggested she thought she would be in trouble. It took many smiles and warm hugs and kisses before Katja realized that our love for her would not change and that, literally, there was no need to cry over spilled milk.

Chapter Eleven

Fast Forward Sixteen Years— We Meet the Birth Parents

From an early age, Katja expressed a keen desire to meet her birth parents. She had two burning questions to resolve, namely: (i) Why did they place her for adoption? and (ii) Did she have any other siblings, especially little sisters? The second question was not surprising, given her twin brothers shared a special bond and at times she felt left out as she did not have her own built-in blood sibling. Unfortunately, I had no concrete answers for her. To address the first question, I felt in the core of my being that her birth parents placed her in the orphanage as a last resort. They would not have had the support available to feed her and provide the necessary surgeries and so had no choice but to leave her with someone who could.

As we went about our daily lives, these questions would surface periodically. Once she reached her twentieth birthday, her need for answers intensified and she was ready to face her past. Katja had now reached a level of maturity that allowed her to accept answers that may have differed from what she was hoping to hear. Therefore, we tried to conduct a bit of research ourselves on the internet. When that went nowhere in a hurry, we considered engaging a private investigator. For a mere $20,000 we could hire an expert with no guarantees about an outcome.

What happened next falls under the category of 'Sometimes the truth is stranger than fiction.' As we were looking for ways to locate Katja's birth parents, my sister decided to gift Katja with a few Ukrainian language lessons as a Christmas present. Given that she teaches English as a second language, she reached out to the international student body at our local university to seek an instructor for Katja. A lovely girl I will refer to as Faith responded, and the language lessons began early in the new year. Imagine our state of shock when we discovered that Faith was from Cherkasy, that same small city Katja called home for her first forty-six months of life!

Over the course of several months, the young ladies met for language lessons and Faith learned more about the adoption story. She became emotionally invested in helping Katja beyond Ukrainian grammar and vocabulary. Meanwhile, Katja was intrigued to meet someone from her hometown.

When the next Christmas rolled around, Faith was returning home to visit her family. She knew about Katja's desire to learn about her birth family and was more than agreeable to do some on-the-ground detective work for us. The only information she had to go on was the address on the original papers filed with the orphanage, completed by her birth parents two decades earlier. We hoped this would provide Faith with a good starting point and sent her off to Ukraine with it and our hopes for some answers.

On the second last evening of that calendar year, Faith and a companion set out to see what they could find at this mysterious address. They came across a series of apartment buildings and knocked on several doors, but to no avail. The information on the form was incomplete, so they were not certain which apartment was the right one. They were about to leave empty-handed when they noticed a ground-floor apartment with its lights on. Why not try one last time? So, on this dark and cold evening in late December, they knocked on the window of this last apartment and an elderly woman responded. The woman demanded to know why Faith and her friend had knocked on her window. Imagine her surprise when she learned that her granddaughter, born two decades years earlier, was alive and lived in Canada! Yes, birth grandma still lived at the address listed on the adoption papers.

Faith and birth grandma called Katja's birth parents, who since moved over 1,000 kilometres away, and shared the shocking news. As it turned out, Katja's birth parents had felt they had no choice at birth but to leave her with the authorities as they were told that she would not survive with them, if at all. They were devastated and moved away to start a new life. So, in answer to Katja's first question, they did indeed leave her at The House of Babies out of love and it was an extremely difficult and life-changing decision for them. They could not even remain in Cherkasy, as it broke their hearts to be reminded about their daughter. At that time, we also learned our answer to the second question. After they had moved away, the couple had two more daughters, which meant Katja does have two younger blood sisters.

I will never forget the look on Katja's face on the morning of December 31. She ran upstairs with wide-eyed enthusiasm to update me with the news that Faith had connected with her birth family. We were stunned about this turn of events. I tried to imagine the shock at the other end, as just knowing Katja was alive would have been astounding for them. More than that, they learned she had been living in Canada all these years and had now showed up on their doorstep—virtually, at least. Faith also sent pictures she had taken of family photographs from the grandmother's apartment. We pored over them for clues and signs of resemblance.

Within days we were connected with Katja's birth parents. We immediately exchanged letters through Google Translate as they spoke no English and my Russian abilities did not extend beyond a few introductory phrases. I explained the story about how we were led to Katja, as well as a bit about her life in Canada. They shared a glimpse of their current lives and discussed the pain involved with their decision to leave Katja at the orphanage. We thanked each other profusely for the role we'd each played in Katja's life.

A few weeks later, we arranged for a Skype call, with Faith present to interpret between the two parties. We were all quite nervous as we dialed in. What would we talk about? Would it be incredibly awkward? As it turned out, poor Faith had her work cut out for her as we conversed back and forth for two hours like long-lost friends. Katja was tongue-tied, so the bulk of the conversation was carried by the four parental figures. Katja looked stunned as she listed to her adoptive and birth parents discuss her right before her eyes.

One question in particular stood out. Katja's birth father questioned why we'd waited so long to seek them out, given we had this address in our possession for sixteen years. It was an excellent question, and the answer was twofold. First, we needed to be certain that Katja was ready to face any reaction that would come from the other side. When she was younger, it would have damaged her to feel rejected again. We had to wait until she was of an age that she could accept any outcome. The other reason was simply one of logistics—we needed to stumble across someone from Cherkasy, Ukraine, who was willing to do a little detective work for us. It was nothing short of a miracle that those two events occurred simultaneously.

I would like to say that we all became one happy family. However, life is messy and rarely that simple. After a flurry of communication, our contact with Katja's birth family waned after a few months. The reality was that they were strangers, we did not speak a common language, and we live a world apart. I will forever be grateful to this beautiful couple who live halfway around the world for giving us the greatest gift one could receive. Katja exchanges pleasantries on birthdays and holidays, but beyond that, she has moved on with her life. Perhaps she will develop a relationship with her younger biological sisters, but that story remains to be written. For now, she received answers to her two burning questions, which helped her to feel at peace with her history, and for that we are extremely pleased.

Another big part of Katja's story is her role as big sister to her twin brothers, Matthew and Nicholas. For this to come to fruition, we again had to hold tight to our family vision and not let the "you can't" people get in our way. To share with you how this all came to be, we must go back to a time shortly after Katja arrived in Canada.

Chapter Twelve

An Unforeseen Phone Call

Following our second trip to Cherkasy to bring Katja home, we enjoyed a few months of summer fun before settling in for our first autumn together as a family. I had just enrolled in MBA classes at McGill, and Dave had resumed a hectic work travel schedule. We continued to attempt pregnancy, as we planned to introduce siblings for Katja, but to no avail. The monthly news, or lack thereof, still disappointed me. At least the intensity of the negative feelings had subsided. Some of my maternal instincts were already met and so that desperate need to get pregnant diminished. We visualized ourselves with more than one child, though, so we anticipated that something was yet to happen.

Life had settled down to this new form of normal when the phone rang. I had no reason to think there was anything unusual about this call that was about to change our lives forever. I answered it to discover our family doctor on the other end. She had supported us through Katja's adoption just five months earlier, and now she was asking me if we were open to another adoption. This was quite a loaded question, so I responded with some articulate answer like, "Um, yeah, of course." I had lots of questions, but instead of keeping me in suspense, she quickly explained.

At that very moment, our doctor had a young girl in her office who was pregnant and looking for options. Shannon (not her real name) expressed that she did not want to put her baby up for adoption through the social services system for two main reasons. First, she would have absolutely no control over the fate of her baby. As soon as she announced publicly her plans to place her child for adoption, the government agencies would have taken control of the situation and decided where her baby would be placed. She likely would not even know the baby's destination for some time, if ever. Secondly, she was aware that the system was not designed to treat her with the utmost respect and dignity by those who should be part of her support group.

In Quebec, this predicament usually meant that the only other viable option available to the birth mother was to abort the baby. At the time, Quebec was the only jurisdiction in North America that did not allow private adoptions. Elsewhere, a birth mother had the privilege of choosing a loving home for her unborn baby. Given the long waiting lists of prospective adoptive parents, she could undoubtedly find what she felt was a suitable home. Although both parties can benefit greatly from this sort of arrangement, Quebec's laws were written to deny any input from the birth mother where her unborn baby is placed. I have not kept up with Quebec adoptions laws over the last two decades, but I certainly hope this has changed to provide birth mothers with more options and control in these circumstances.

Angels

Our story would not be complete without a shout-out to the angels that were placed in our path along the way of our family-building saga. You already met Faith. I mean, what are the odds that a girl from Cherkasy would answer my sister's request for a Ukrainian-speaking tutor for Katja? This one was clear to me, even at the time, but I believe there were instances in which we were not even aware of the celestial help we received. For you doubters, I am going to take you back to Switzerland for another distinct example before coming back to the present.

My faith in angels was strengthened the day after my miscarriage, during our final few days in Europe. I had just returned days earlier from the hospital and now our apartment bustled with the men who were packing our furniture. They were preparing for our move to Montreal the very next day. While I was crippled by emotional and physical pain, so many scattered thoughts fought for attention in my head. Just a couple of days earlier, I had a clear picture of what my new life would be in Montreal. We would arrive as I entered my fifth month of pregnancy and so I could concentrate on building our nest until our little bundle arrived. Suddenly, I was not pregnant, I was grieving, and I had no job prospects. I was both confused and frustrated.

Despite my internal angst, the movers obliviously proceeded with their duties. As they worked, I moped around the apartment, trying to clear my head and make sense out of life. It was a moment when I had to separate my mind from the reality of what my physical body had to do so I could get through the day. In between answering the movers' multitude of questions—in French, nonetheless—I could feel the walls closing in on me and my tears stung as they tried to escape my eyes. Finally, I had to leave the movers and wander around our little town of Nyon. I had no destination in mind. I just needed somewhere I could walk aimlessly and sob uncontrollably without anyone disturbing me.

I did not care who saw me. I just openly cried as I walked through the town. I stopped by our church, which was situated just around the corner from our apartment. I tried to open the doors but was disappointed to discover they were locked. Nobody was around. I prayed to God to please send me an angel. I felt I did not have the strength to deal with the activities and emotions on that particular day without the physical presence of someone to support me.

I knew that my pity party would have to end, because there was a lot of work to be done to clean up our apartment in a short amount of time. The shipping container to Montreal would not wait until I was in a better mood to pack our belongings. So, after some time, I decided it was time to return to our increasingly empty apartment to answer the questions the movers had stored up for me.

Within minutes of my return, the doorbell rang. It was our minister's wife, Pauline, who'd stopped by to see if I needed some comfort. She had arrived a few minutes earlier, but she left when the movers explained I was gone, and they did not know when I would return. For some reason, Pauline had a strong sense that she needed to circle back and try again. My angel came back for me! We went for a quick coffee and she let me pour out my emotions before her. She shared invaluable words of encouragement. At the end of our conversation, I knew I had the strength to get through the day. Pauline had never been to our apartment before that day. I do not believe that she accidentally showed up when I desperately needed some comfort. I had prayed for an angel at that specific moment and my prayer was answered.

Similarly, I believe it was an angel that led us to our doctor in Montreal. Some might argue that her placement in our lives at this time was a mere coincidence. I believe that we were meant to cross paths with our angel at the exact moment in time that we did, so that our worlds would collide with Shannon's when she visited the doctor on that fateful day.

You see, it was a very thin thread that led us to our doctor, and therefore to Shannon. The story is too good to pass up, so we have to travel back in time again so I can explain. In our final weeks in Switzerland, we met a husband and wife who were new to our community. He was a diplomat, and his wife was from our home province of Saskatchewan. It was such a brief encounter that I cannot even remember our angel's name. The discussion lasted long enough for her to learn that I was pregnant, and that we were moving to Montreal. Therefore, she mentioned to me that her childhood friend was a doctor in the greater Montreal area and had a big heart for her patients. I assumed that in a city of three million people, I would seek a referral to a doctor close to our house, which would be handy through our pregnancy and beyond. So, I scribbled down the contact information on a napkin and tucked it away for another day.

After we settled into our new home in Montreal a few months later, Dave and I began our new life and enjoyed the wonderful activities the vibrant city had to offer. Before long, I knew I would need to find a doctor as our family expansion project continued but with no results. I recalled that somewhere I had a doctor's name and phone number scribbled on a napkin. I was a little troubled that I only had the home phone number. How would a big-city doctor react to a prospective patient calling her at home to make an appointment?

For several moments, I considered merely calling another

doctor in the phone book (remember those?). This course of action would allow me to not only find a doctor in close proximity to our house, but it would also provide me with the office number. I sat on the bed, phone in hand, and worked through this dilemma. In the end, the attraction of a personal referral pushed me to call this stranger at home. I vividly recall feeling a sense of relief when this unknown doctor answered my call warmly and immediately put me at ease. We chatted like old friends and, as we were winding down our conversation, I requested a referral to a doctor in our neighbourhood. She inquired where we lived and imagine my surprise when she said her office was within a few minutes of our house!

Meeting a doctor for a first appointment can be awkward, but I felt like I had known this one for years. I brought her up to date in our lives and explained our lack of success in the baby department. We had started to entertain the idea of Katja's adoption and so I shared that with her, as well. Our new doctor led us through the infertility testing battle while simultaneously following the progress we were making in our quest to adopt Katja. When we needed help to bring Katja home, she was one of the numerous people who sent a letter to Immigration Canada on our behalf. She cheered with us when we brought Katja home and was as relieved as we were when she gave Katja a clean bill of health. Within a short time, our new doctor had become an integral part of our lives. Her role was about to get even bigger.

Throughout this first year in Montreal, I learned about the numerous adoption cases initiated by our doctor. I discovered that she wanted to provide pregnant girls an option that the social system did not support. Within the confines of the law, she found a way to go one step further to help her patients.

Immediately on the heels of an appointment with a distraught pregnant girl, another patient would come through the doors who desperately wanted to conceive a child, just like us. It became apparent that a logical solution would be to play matchmaker to the two parties. Our doctor was able to find a way to do that which didn't jeopardize her professional standing. All she did was provide the birth mother with a phone number of a potential adoptive party who, despite their best efforts, had so far been unable to realize their family goals. If she chose to do so, the birth mother would meet with the individual or couple. The birth mother controlled whether that initial phone call was even placed. If the two parties did meet to discuss a potential adoption, the birth mother determined the outcome.

You may wonder why a busy doctor would bother matching up the two parties if private adoptions were not even allowed. Well, there was a bit of an oddity to the law at the time. While a birth mother did not have the privilege of deciding where her unborn baby would be placed, for some reason she did have this luxury for a child that was already born. Furthermore, there was nothing in the laws that prevented the birth mother from making this decision the moment the baby entered the world. So, as long as the paperwork was not filed until after the birth, the adoption could function like a private placement.

I believe that a private adoption arrangement can prove advantageous for all parties. The birth mother leaves the hospital with a sense of relief and comfort, knowing she has placed the baby in good hands. In each of the adoptions previously initiated by our doctor, the birth mothers never wavered from their position and felt at peace with their decision throughout the process. Not surprisingly, it is more common for a birth mother to change her mind to keep her baby in the final hour if she has no idea or input into who will raise the baby that she carried the past nine months.

The adoptive couple clearly benefits from a private adoption, as they are blessed with a long-awaited baby.

Before we moved to Montreal, our doctor had facilitated a dozen of these meetings that ultimately led to successful adoptions. After providing the birth mother with the phone number, she would step aside and let the courts take over. Without exception, lawyers were involved from the beginning in order to ensure all processes were conducted within legal requirements. We were assured by our lawyer that, as long as no money exchanged hands and all papers were filed in the courts after the birth, the adoption would be perfectly legal. If we had to play out this charade to save the life of our child, then so be it.

The Meeting

Before leaping to any conclusions about what this surprise phone call from our doctor could mean for us, I had to consult with Dave to see if he had any strong reaction either way. I desperately wanted to meet Shannon, and I was reasonably sure he would agree with me. Still, I was especially eager to reach him that day, which was problematic as he was overseas on business. I left a message calmly asking him to return my call. So, like me, Dave unsuspectingly made what he thought was a routine call.

After a quick, "Hi, honey, how is your day?" I asked the loaded question. I braced myself for an analysis of the pros and cons of such a prospect, in case my husband wanted to be logical about this. Sometimes, when Dave senses I am emotionally charged in a situation, he takes it upon himself to bring me down to earth so I don't get my hopes up. This is to protect me from my strong emotions, but it was too late. (As an aside, I think the phrase "don't get your hopes up" is absurd. Without hope, what kind of a dismal existence would we have?) My hopes were already soaring, and I was optimistic he would throw caution to the wind and agree to meet with Shannon without reservation. To my relief, this was the case. I wasted no time in making the arrangements.

Dave was scheduled to return to Canada the next day, so Shannon and I decided we would meet at our home two days later. I tried not to obsess about the impending meeting too much, as she had not made any commitments at that stage. It was not even certain she would follow through with the pregnancy. I fruitlessly tried my best to maintain some detachment, but still found myself both excited and nervous as I contemplated how important this meeting would be in the whole scheme of our lives. Either Shannon would like us and decide that she wanted us to adopt her baby, or she would not like us and place her baby elsewhere or terminate her pregnancy. The stakes were very high.

As scheduled, the doorbell rang, and we were suddenly face to face with the person who had the power to grant us a life. She came prepared, and so, after some nervous small talk, she started to screen us. Dave and I were both impressed with the maturity and thoroughness of her questions. Clearly, she wanted to be comfortable that this baby would go to a home filled with happiness, love, and stability.

Her questions ranged from our views on diverse topics including discipline and homosexuality. She had a long list to get through and we answered each one as honestly and completely as we could, as this was an arrangement that would be solely based on trust. Until after the birth, there would be no legal documents or standard protocols to follow. We would have to rely on each other's word to fulfill pledges made at the outset. So, we set the tone with complete honesty and sincerity in our answers.

Shannon appreciated our candour. After two hours, we parted

company. I did not know how she felt at that point, but I knew I was instantly committed to this adoption. I could not sleep as the possibilities swirled through my head. Dave was much more cautious than I was and preferred to wait and see what happened. Although he was trying to keep me from a big disappointment, it was too late. If Shannon did not choose us, I would have felt a great loss that would have been akin to our miscarriage.

Yet Another Important Phone Call

In recounting our story, it has struck me how often our lives were greatly affected by the simple ring of a telephone. This was prior to the pervasiveness of texting. My nerves were raw the next morning when the phone rang, and I answered the call to discover Shannon on the other end. She could not have already made her decision as she had left our house mere hours before.

As it turned out, this time she simply called to inquire if she had left a personal item at our house. I do not recall what the item was, but I remember feeling relieved to hear her voice as it provided assurance to me that I had not imagined the entire meeting. As our doctor was interested in the outcome of our meeting, I telephoned her and mentioned this surprise phone call that was placed the very next day. When I told her about this conversation, she intuited that Shannon's call was significant. She felt that, perhaps on a subconscious level, Shannon also wanted to ensure that she had not imagined the meeting.

Fortunately, we only had to wait two days before Shannon called to officially ask us to be the adoptive parents of her baby. Without a moment's hesitation, we said yes! We knew that we had to overcome several steps, but at least none of them would involve Immigration Canada, and for this I was very grateful. This time, the biggest risk was that Shannon would change her mind at any point, as we could not even begin any paperwork until after the birth of the baby. We would have absolutely no recourse if Shannon called one day and said that she had made a mistake and she did not want us to adopt her baby. The other significant risk we faced was that our little secret would be revealed, causing social services to crash our party and take over custody of our baby.

There was no way to mitigate these two risks, as lessening one resulted in an instant increase to the other. For example, we could not defend ourselves against Shannon changing her mind throughout the adoption without filing any legal papers with the court. However, by publicizing our plan to adopt this baby, we would have lost our very ability to adopt, as the baby would have become the ward of social services. The best we could do was keep quiet and wait. These are not my areas of strength.

At least I was much more prepared for cautiously optimistic reactions when we announced our second adoption. Not surprisingly, our support group was unanimous in believing the number-one cause for concern was that Shannon would change her mind. My gut instinct was that she would not, and I could only hope I was right. I tried to relay to others who had not met Shannon that this was a girl who was confident with her decision. Even though she was young, she had a wisdom and maturity beyond her years.

My coat of armour was virtually impenetrable by this point and so I was unfazed to hear multiple stories of almost-private adoptions. I was already aware of the multitude of heartbreaking cases of prospective adoptive parents who had their intended child ripped from under them at the last minute. I can only imagine the heartbreak and disappointment of such an event. Several years later, I met a birth mother who changed her mind at the final hour, and I could feel her anguish when hearing the story from her perspective. Throughout Shannon's entire pregnancy, I was able to keep faith that our dream would come true.

The greatest irony I found at this stage of the adoption was the concern expressed by Shannon's support group that *we* would be the ones to change our minds. They were worried that, in the end, Shannon would be forced to face the social services process she so desperately wanted to avoid. Shannon and I compared notes about the opposing feedback we were receiving. We mutually consoled each other that our friends and family, while entirely well-intentioned, were wrong. Shannon, Dave, and I were completely committed to this adoption.

Another interesting observation is that I had less concerns about the pregnancy spontaneously terminating than when I was pregnant myself. In my own case, I was continuously aware of any sign that could indicate a miscarriage. Perhaps because I had absolutely no control over the pregnancy in this situation, I did not stress about Shannon miscarrying, other than for the brief moment I will describe below. We were fully aware that other potential barriers lay ahead, and so I did not entertain that a miscarriage could be one of them.

The only moment that I had to face the threat of a miscarriage occurred approximately two weeks after we met Shannon, when she called me to tell me she had experienced some spotting. For a brief moment I wondered if this dream would be realized. In that split second of thinking the pregnancy might be at risk, I realized just how committed I was to our unborn baby emotionally. The sinking feeling instantly reminded me of how I felt at the time of my own miscarriage. This incident clearly proved to me that the attachment one feels does not require a physical reality of pregnancy. I was already emotionally attached to that baby, whether there was a physical bond yet or not.

One Final Request

When Shannon asked us to adopt her baby, she asked me for one more favour. I said, "Sure," but braced myself. My mind raced as I imagined what she would need from me that would not hinder the adoption plans. I did not lose sight of the fact that this woman would be giving us the gift of life, so I would have jumped through a hoop of fire if she had asked me to. Luckily, her request was not nearly as dangerous.

Shannon asked me to participate as the birth coach. She wanted me to attend doctor appointments with her, participate in pre-natal classes, and assist at the birth. I was flabbergasted and thrilled at the same time. I would be one of the first to see our baby enter the world. I would be one of the first people to hold the new bundle. I would not have to wait around for yet another significant phone call to advise us that our baby had been born. Beyond that, I was honoured that Shannon felt comfortable enough to allow me into such an intimate process. I was aware that this would strengthen a bond between Shannon and me that would be difficult to break when we parted ways, but the benefits of this arrangement outweighed the risks. Without hesitation, I agreed to her request.

Chapter Thirteen

Preparation for Baby . . . Babies?!

C ompleting Katja's adoption required a lot of activity on my part. As challenging as it was, I could control our progression throughout the long process. In preparing for our second adoption, I could do little more than simply wait, which provided a different type of challenge. My role as the birth coach was fortunate, as it gave me a purpose and something to do in the interim. As for paperwork, there was only one document to prepare, and it was one we already knew well.

One of the first items I researched after Shannon asked us to adopt her baby was the home study. We could not leverage our previous home study as it was only valid for one year. Besides, a different procedure is followed for local adoptions and so a separate home study was required no matter what.

This time the home study was a little challenging to arrange as we could not announce our specific plans to adopt the baby of a young lady we knew to be pregnant. All we could do was declare that we intended to adopt again soon (which was true) and so needed an update to our home study (also true). While the home study process for Katja's adoption was vividly etched in my memory, I can barely remember even meeting with the social worker for our second study. There are three significant reasons for this.

First, the update to the initial study was much less involved. Fewer meetings were required and fewer questions were asked. So, this process was less memorable because I had expected it to be more complicated than it was. We were pleasantly surprised when our social worker announced we had just completed our final meeting as I had anticipated more. Throughout our journey, I discovered that I tended to remember the unpleasant surprises more than the pleasant ones and this was definitely of the latter form. The lesson learned here is that setting appropriate expectations can help to avoid disappointment. I found that simultaneously setting appropriate expectations while keeping my hopes up was a challenge!

The abbreviated process relates directly to my second point, which is that the second home study came at a significantly reduced rate. As we were required to pay the social workers on an hourly basis, fewer meetings and a shorter report meant less cash outflow. This was another positive surprise and one that may have even gone unnoticed had I not been documenting our journey. These minor positive outcomes need to be celebrated.

Finally, the biggest difference of all was that our second home study did not lie on the critical path of our adoption. We could not even use the document until after the birth, so it did not matter if the process took several months to complete. On the other hand, Katja's adoption progress depended on the completion, legalization, and translation of documents, so any delay in the home study meant a direct delay in completing the adoption. I was pleasantly surprised when this home study was completed more quickly than anticipated.

The only other document we were required to sign was one that I could prepare myself. In order to ensure the adoption was legal, we had to provide written confirmation that no money had exchanged hands. This was one of the laws that made perfect sense to me. The government wanted to ensure that no parties were entering into adoption agreements to exploit the children for profit. Typically, once money enters the adoption system, such as it does in developing countries, it is hard to keep the system free from corruption. Other than paying for any costs directly associated with the pregnancy and delivery, no payment may be made to either the birth mother or a third party, and I was happy to attest to that.

And Then There Were Two

I was very pleased when Shannon invited me along to her doctor and ultrasound appointments. These outings were very positive for me on multiple levels. First, they allowed me to personally experience a full-term pregnancy as much as possible. It was a gift to participate and witness first-hand the thrill of watching the evolution of a tiny embryo into a newborn baby. I remembered the ultrasound during my own pregnancy, and how exciting it was to see the little heart beating inside the blob of a form the technician assured me was the beginnings of a baby. This excitement escalates as the pregnancy advances, and I was privileged to directly encounter all of these emotions.

Another advantage to participating in these appointments was that Katja was able to witness this side of adoption. As she watched

Shannon's stomach grow throughout the months, she better understood that her baby brother or sister was also growing. Our next-door neighbour was expecting at exactly the same time, so we had a golden opportunity to explain to Katja that some babies grow inside the tummy of the mom that raises them, and some do not. (Side trivia – our neighbour's son, also named Matthew, was born on the exact same day as our twins – 7 minutes after our Matthew and 20 minutes before Nicholas!)

I recalled hearing some excellent advice that if ever an adopted child remembers the moment that they were told they were adopted, the parents waited too long to tell them. I never wanted to surprise our children with such news. And besides, the story of how we came to be a family is one to celebrate, not hide.

The pregnancy was progressing normally. Late in January, midway through the second trimester, Katja and I met Shannon at the hospital for the first scheduled ultrasound. We had just begun marveling at the picture on the screen when the technician very calmly asked, "You knew you were having twins, didn't you?" And that was how we found out we were not adopting one child. We were adopting two!

Shannon and I looked at each other with wide eyes. She told the technician that she had no idea, and many thoughts were running through both of our heads. I desperately wanted to get to a phone and call Dave, but I could not appear too anxious, as I was merely the friend along for the appointment. I did not find this out until after, but Shannon's initial concern was that this news could cause us to change our minds. Such a thought could not have been further from the truth and I was ecstatic with the news, but she did not know this at the time. I was excited, nervous, and happy all at once. After the technician left the room, Shannon and I looked at each other with our mouths gaping open, while exchanging and repeating "I can't believe it!"

I knew that Dave would never renege on the adoption because of this news. We were as committed to this pregnancy as if it were me actually carrying the baby (babies). After all, in the case of a natural pregnancy, one does not pre-order the birth results and this was no different. On a logical level, I knew that Dave understood these points as well. I just hoped that, emotionally, he was as excited about this news as I was. More specifically, I was hoping that he would look on it as the incredible gift that I saw, and not with a dread about the extra cost, time, or energy this little news update would drain from us.

I was kept in suspense because, once again, Dave was overseas on a business trip in London on the day we received the news. Due to his schedule and the difference in time zones, I was unable to reach him all day. With many extraneous thoughts running through my head, I made it through a finance exam I had that evening and then finally reached him during the break. This time, I was successful. He started to tell me about his day before I interrupted him with the events of my day that I was certain were much more interesting than anything he had to say.

I felt as though everyone in the hallways could hear my heart beating loudly as I prepared for his reaction. However, there was not a moment's hesitation on Dave's part when he said, "Wow, that is so cute!" I remember his words well because cute is not a word Dave would typically use. I think he, too, was a little stunned. In a good way. Not once did my accountant husband point out that we would need to pay for (and change) twice as many diapers. Had he known how expensive formula was, as well as how hungry our two babies would be, he may have commented that this news was going to send us crawling to the bank. But he didn't. Even if he predicted how exhausted we would be in the first months, he did not let on. His reaction was one of surprise and excitement.

After the phone call with Dave, I finally allowed myself to believe and rejoice in the news. I had said many times in my life that I would love to have twins and now my dream was coming true. Having twins meant that Shannon would have more appointments and be under a slightly closer watch. Otherwise, the same routine carried on for the rest of the pregnancy.

As Shannon's birth coach, I took my place in the prenatal classes along with the partners. I was the breathing-helper, the muscle-massager, the encourager, and the one who would try to keep busy, even though there would really be nothing useful I could do when the actual labour took place. Even with the lack of practical application for much of what was learned in the prenatal classes, the whole process was a valuable experience. In particular, I believe prenatal classes encourage partners who might not actively participate to become involved in the birth. I also believe they help the birth mothers, who have many questions and can receive some reassurances from the instructor and videos.

In our situation, the prenatal classes provided us with a unique opportunity to share a closeness under the extremely unusual circumstances that had brought us together. We both knew that an emotionally difficult time lay ahead for Shannon, but by staying distracted with appointments and classes, we were able to avoid this thought when we were together. Nobody in the class knew our situation and everyone just presumed that Shannon's family friend was there to support her.

In between appointments and classes, Dave, Katja, and I went on living our normal lives. We enjoyed our first fall with our daughter. We travelled north of Montreal to visit a friend's acreage, where Katja experienced the joys of jumping into a pile of leaves.

Then the leaves were covered by snow and she enjoyed digging tunnels and making snowmen. We celebrated our first Christmas together in Western Canada, surrounded by our extended families. Katja continued making friends at her daycare, as well as in the neighbourhood. Dave was traveling a lot and I persevered with my classes at McGill. We were living a relatively peaceful existence for the time being as we awaited the birth of our twins.

My Own Labour Pains

Around mid-May, I began to feel a piercing, shooting pain all the way through my right leg. I assumed I had overdone my last workout, and so tried to ignore it. Instead of diminishing over time, the pain became increasingly intense. Then my leg started to swell on the Saturday of the long weekend in May, which was quite inconvenient timing. I decided that when our doctor's office reopened on Tuesday, I would make an appointment to find the source of the pain and swelling.

This seemed like a good plan until that same day when my temperature rapidly started climbing and I could not even get out of bed. I started to become nervous, as I was cognizant enough to realize that the high fever was making me dizzy. We took my temperature and were surprised to see it had risen to 105 degrees Fahrenheit. We called a neighbour, who happened to be a nurse, and she told me not to delay any further—I needed to get to a hospital and not wait until after the weekend to see our doctor.

Immediately Dave literally dragged me to the outpatient clinic, as my leg was too sore to even move. I was more annoyed at the inconvenience than worried about what could be happening in my body. Since we were so close to the birth of the twins, I did not think that I had time to spare for an unplanned visit to the clinic, but the pain motivated me to go anyway. This turned out to be a good decision. The warmth of spring had arrived, so I was able to wear loose shorts instead of trying to pull a pair of pants over my leg that was now swollen to double its regular size. I was not content with the regular size of my leg, but after seeing it this swollen, I was eager to get my original leg back!

We arrived at the hospital and waited. Finally, my number was called. The doctor took one quick look at my leg, glanced at my temperature reading, and immediately sent me across the street to the hospital emergency. He told me not to go home first, as he suspected my condition was something quite serious. He did not divulge any more information other than to warn me that I might be invited for an extended stay at the hospital. This was a bit worrisome as I could not envision spending my first days of mothering newborn twins from a hospital bed. We followed the doctor's instructions and headed to the hospital. I was in such a state of pain and delirium that I would have agreed to anything the doctor said to make it go away.

At least I was not required to wait long for my second examination. Almost immediately upon entering the hospital, I was assigned a doctor. Within a few moments, the doctor diagnosed me with cellulitis. At first, I thought he was trying to insult me. Before this experience, the only cellulite I heard of, while not pleasant, was not a life-threatening condition. As he explained my condition to me, I became less indignant.

I found out that what I had was the precursor to flesh-eating disease. Without the proper care, patients with this condition lose limbs, if not their lives. The treatment prescribed to me was a very strong antibiotic that had to be administered twice daily through an intravenous needle. They needed to begin my first treatment right away. The nurses gently inserted the intravenous needle into the top of my hand, and I settled in for my first dose of antibiotic. I was relieved to receive medication, even though it would still be a matter of days before I could walk normally again. Expecting an indefinite hospital stay, I was thankful when the nurses informed me that I would be able to return home in between treatments. I simply had to return to the hospital every morning and evening for a thirty-minute treatment.

Coincidentally, these treatments occurred at the same hospital where Shannon's obstetrician practised, as well as the hospital to which she would be admitted when she went into labour. I called Shannon immediately to tell her about my condition. Since we were nearing the end of the pregnancy, it was especially important that she be able to reach me at all times.

Shannon was now scheduled for weekly appointments at the hospital. So, after my Wednesday morning treatment, we met for her appointment and then I was scheduled for more tests that day. The doctors were concerned about the continued swelling in my leg, and they wanted to check for blood clots. I will not dwell on the details but suffice it to say that these were the most painful tests I had undergone to date in my life. I knew I was in for a long haul when they told me not to be too shy to scream out loud.

That was a long day. I had been in the hospital since my intravenous appointment at 8 a.m., and it was now late in the afternoon. I sat alone in excruciating pain as I waited for test results, hoping they would not find out something terrible was happening to my body. Through the pain and frustration, it occurred to me that perhaps this ordeal was meant to be my version of labour pains. It helped get through this awful day to think that it was all for a higher purpose. I also realized that I was lucky to be incapacitated when I was, and not after the babies were born. We knew they were due soon, but I did not realize that we would meet our sons even sooner than we thought. As I sat stewing in my thoughts, the good news arrived that the antibiotics were working and so I would fortunately not require an alternative and more aggressive form of treatment.

Dave and Katja picked me up around 6 p.m. I was so happy to escape the hospital . . . until I had to return two hours later for my evening treatment. At the end of this awful day, I finally noticed that my leg was ever so slightly responding to the medication. I had just completed Day 4 of the treatments and there was a slight decrease in the pain and swelling. This timing was fortuitous, because early the very next morning, we would again receive one of those phone calls that would change our lives forever.

Chapter Fourteen

Return to the Hospital

We were startled out of our sleep early Thursday morning by the shrill ring of the phone. Early morning calls usually signify momentous events, and this was no exception. Shannon's water had broken, and her mother was about to drive her to the hospital. I arranged to meet them on the labour and delivery ward as soon as my morning antibiotic treatment was completed.

That particular thirty-minute treatment seemed longer than the previous eight sessions. Once the medication started to take effect, my condition improved quickly and so I was just anxious for the real events of the day to begin. Although my presence in Shannon's room would not induce labour, I felt that in my absence, I was missing out on precious moments.

I did not know what to anticipate, but I expected to walk into a dramatic scene playing out in Shannon's room. In the movies, we witness hysteria and heightened emotions before, during, and after a birth. So, why was Shannon sitting calmly in the room? There must be something wrong, I thought, as no doctors or nurses were even in sight. Nobody else seemed distressed, so I decided to relax and enjoy every moment of the experience.

It didn't take long before Shannon started to experience pain. We passed the time by pacing up and down the corridor. I imagined we made quite the pair, me limping alongside Shannon as she took cautious steps with great discomfort. We had matching intravenous needles sprouting out of our hands. We were both in pain and anxious about the upcoming hours.

To help combat Shannon's discomfort, we reverted to the exercises we had learned in the prenatal classes. But, as I had predicted, they did nothing other than briefly distract Shannon from the pain. Also, for a few moments, I felt useful. I must admit that when the doctor gave Shannon the epidural, I silently prayed a word of thanks that I played the supporting role in this drama.

Around noon, the intense labour began, and the doctor arrived to commence his work. Shannon's mother and I continued our fruitless attempts to make her comfortable. I also continued to play out my strange role in a surreal play. Mentally, I watched myself assist this woman who I had only known for seven months give birth to our babies. Although I was continually cognizant that the babies I was about to hold would be my responsibility for life, it would not be until I saw their physical presence that the reality of what that meant really hit me.

To witness the birth of our twins was a gift for me. I watched intently as the first head made its entry into our world. At precisely 1:20 p.m., Twin #1 was born. Then Shannon endured more pushing and labour. Later, we would discover that Twin #2 was lying per-pendicular to the birth canal, and so the doctors and nurses were concerned that he would not engage himself in time. I thought that we had an extra audience of nurses and doctors because they were excited to witness the birth of twins. In reality, they were prepared to take Shannon into the next room at a moment's notice to perform an emergency caesarian section.

Luckily, surgery was not necessary. Twenty-seven minutes later, at 1:47 p.m., I watched Twin #2 enter this world. Wow! What a thrill! The nurses were a bit uneasy with the first twin's colouring and so had whisked him away. We had all been distracted and so did not even learn about the details until after the second birth. All that mattered now was that everyone was back in the room and it was all over. Or, shall I say, it had just begun.

Immediately, the nurses asked Shannon if she had chosen the names of the babies. Obviously, the staff did not know that Dave and I would choose their names. We had already decided that Twin #1 would be Matthew David. As for Twin #2, we had a few names picked out, but had not confirmed them before the birth. So, I discreetly shook my head at Shannon, and she told the nurse they would have to wait another day for his name. We would confirm Nicholas Joshua the very next day.

I was so honoured to have experienced the birth of our babies, and even more overjoyed to hold them in the first few minutes of their precious lives. I have spoken with many mothers of newborns who feel a sense of overwhelming joy, mixed with a sense of total responsibility, and my feelings were no different.

Two Long Days

As this was a birth of multiples, the doctors wanted to observe Shannon and the babies for an additional night. This was a difficult time for everyone involved, as we were still not free to discuss our adoption plans with the hospital staff. Had we done so, we would have presented them with a dilemma—keep our secret and risk losing their professional careers, or else blow the whistle on us and break the hearts of Shannon, Dave, and me plus change the course of the twins' lives in a completely random and unknown direction.

We found out later that, perhaps, we had not been quite as discreet as we had thought. Two weeks after leaving the hospital, Shannon returned for a follow-up appointment, at which time the obstetrician inquired about the twins. By this point, it was safe to inform him that the twins were being adopted as we had officially and openly begun the proceedings. When she did, one of the doctors deadpanned, "Oh, to the woman in the delivery room with you?" There was no hint of surprise with the question, which signaled to me that some of the staff might have suspected what was happening. I could only guess that they felt it was not in anyone's best interests to sabotage the arrangement. We couldn't agree more.

So, as long as Shannon and the twins still remained in the hospital, we had to be extremely discreet. I wanted to be with them every moment to soak up time with our new boys and learn what I could while in the protective surroundings of the hospital. It was a privilege for me to be able to bathe the twins for the first time in their lives. They both had such spindly legs that I could not believe they would ever be able to support their weight. I learned at bathtime, though, not to underestimate their strength.

All I had to do was lift them out of a wire-framed bassinet one at a time and insert them into the portable plastic bathtub. I did not think a one-day-old baby would be much competition for me. After all, I had been working out and felt quite fit. My intention was to bathe Matthew first; however, he had decided otherwise and grabbed onto the metal bars of the bassinet. He would not let go. I would pry one hand off and then the other would latch on. In the end, I won (using all of my strength and both hands), though I realized I had just met my match!

While I did not want to miss a single moment of this precious time, I also felt it was important to allow Shannon time to say goodbye, with the support of her family around her. Our own support group found this arrangement troublesome, as we had no guarantees that we would leave the hospital with our sons. Dave and I felt secure about the outcome. We had a sense of peace and calm about us throughout the entire process. Nonetheless, the two days passed slowly, as we were eager to begin this new chapter in our lives.

Katja Meets Her New Brothers

Having two live dolls catered directly to Katja's maternal instincts. On the day following their birth, I asked if she would like to come to the hospital to meet Matthew and Nicholas and she responded with a hearty "yes!"

Shannon and her family had grown very fond of Katja, and so I was comfortable bringing Katja into this unorthodox situation. She understood, on some level, that Shannon had carried Matthew and Nicholas in her tummy and soon we would take them home to begin their lives with us. We let Katja hold the twins and she proved to be a natural big sister. At the end of the second afternoon, we all said goodbye to the twins for the last time.

I remember clearly our last afternoon with Katja as our only child physically with us. We were driving home from our second-last hospital visit when we came upon the grand opening of a store. To help celebrate (and advertise), the owners were throwing an outdoor party. We knew this was a good opportunity to give Katja the last chance for undivided attention she would receive for a while. Dave parked the car and escorted Katja down the giant blow-up slide a few times. We enjoyed the beautiful, sunny day, while we munched on hot dogs and drank soda. After we had enough, we returned home for our last restful night in a long time.

I took advantage of this calm before the storm to prepare the first batch of the many bottles I would make over the coming months. I thought sixteen bottles seemed like a lot, but quickly realized this was merely a one-day supply. I had already packed the bag we would need to take to the hospital the next day. Matthew and Nicholas's cribs were ready, and their clothes awaited them in their drawers and closet. I also thought I had sufficiently stocked up on a few packages of diapers, once again thinking I was set for a while. Nobody informed me that newborns do not take regular bathroom breaks every few hours. I had to discover on my own that the bathroom habits of a newborn are comparable to that of a slow and steady leak.

Another Pick-Up

On the morning of May 29, two days after Matthew and Nicholas entered this world, Dave and I set off for the hospital to bring our sons home. We left Katja at home with a babysitter, as we knew this would be a difficult and emotional farewell.

We walked into Shannon's hospital room and were greeted by her mother. Shannon was completing the hospital release forms. Upon her return to the room, we waited for the doctor to officially release Shannon and the twins from the hospital. Having shared such closeness over the last seven months, I found myself making nervous small talk with Shannon. There was nothing we could do except await the arrival of the attending physician. All bags were packed, and we knew what role we each had to play. Finally, the doctor relieved our tension, as he made his rounds into our room to officially release Shannon and the twins from the hospital. I could only imagine what went through Shannon's mind at this time, and I credit her for her bravery as she methodically picked up her bags and played her part out to the end.

We made the long trek down the hallway. I felt as though the hospital staff were watching us intently, as if they knew what was transpiring. If anyone knew what was about to happen after we shut the doors behind us, they never let on. I waited for someone to stop us, but nobody did. The door opened and we all walked into the bright sunshine. Dave and I drove Shannon to the parking lot across the street. Ironically, we returned to the parking lot of our mutual doctor's office. The irony of saying goodbye where the story all began did not escape me.

We wanted to make this moment as painless as possible, as there were many goodbyes to be said that day. I knew that after we left the hospital grounds, my relationship with Shannon would instantly change. We would always share a bond, but we would go from having regular communication and sharing many close moments to almost a complete break in contact. We would still need to make arrangements to complete the legal agreements; however, seeing Shannon face to face again was now doubtful as it would be too painful for her.

It was hard for everyone concerned, except the twins. They were completely oblivious to this turning point in their lives. From my point of view, I again reverted to the survival technique of desensitizing myself by pretending I was watching myself from above. Before we went our separate ways, many tears were shed, and we all endured a few grueling, emotional moments. Then, Dave and I were left alone to buckle our new sons in their car seats and bring them to their new family home.

Private Adoption—Is It For You?

Despite the emotional toll it takes on the adults involved, private adoptions can be a great solution to that basic supply and demand problem alluded to previously. For a pregnant girl who does not feel equipped to be a mother, the supply of babies exceeds her demand. On the other hand, for potential adoptive parents who either want to begin or supplement a family through adoption, demand exceeds supply. When you match two such parties, a win-win equilibrium is created.

Private adoptions provide the birth mother with a certain degree of control over her situation. Keeping her baby may not be feasible and, adopting the baby out through social services may not be palatable. As the one who selects the adoptive family, she can leave the hospital with peace of mind that she has placed the baby she carried for nine months in a loving and stable home. To our knowledge, Shannon never wavered from her decision to place the babies with us. She clearly affirmed to me that her security in the arrangement hinged on the fact that it was *she* who *chose* us.

In addition to control, Shannon also wanted to maintain her dignity throughout the process and her impression was that this may not have been possible if she chose the social services route. Clearly, one would not claim that every case worker will fail to meet the needs of every birth mother, but the birth mother's perception of mistreatment could be enough to convince her to end the pregnancy rather than endure becoming just another case. Private adoptive parents have the opportunity to bestow on the birth mother of their future child the respect she deserves. After all, she is the conduit through which they are about to realize their dreams of a family. They need to recognize and fully appreciate her bravery. We sure did.

Chapter Fifteen

Another Court Appearance

The very next day, I found myself initiating yet another unusual phone call. I was not sure where to begin, but I knew that, somehow, I had to inform social services that we had twin three-day old babies at home with us that were ours to adopt. The initial reaction of the administrator on the other end was "you can't do that." Luckily, I had heard that reaction before and so was unfazed as I ignored it and pressed forward to ask how we could make it happen.

The woman on the other end was well-versed in her job, as she knew that this was an unusual request. She must have thought I had not thought of this earlier, but she enlightened me that I could have brought this to their attention before the babies were born. I responded that I was well aware of that fact, but then Shannon would have no control over where the babies went. The woman confirmed this and then I realized that she'd missed the point completely. She could not grasp that we had only chosen this path so that Shannon could purposely place the twins with us for adoption.

It did not really matter if the woman on the other end of the call ever did understand our motivation. We continued our discussion about how to sort through the required steps to turn this impossibility into a reality. There was never a question of *if* it would work; I just needed to know *how*. She informed me that we would need an updated home study, to which I promptly replied that we had already completed this step. The next step was to randomly select from a list one of the unfamiliar lawyers' names who could help us finalize the process. Pretty easy compared to Katja's adoption.

Still, we were accurately warned that the most difficult for us would be to endure the waiting period. We filed the initial papers and then could do nothing further until four months had passed. During this period, Shannon had the legal right to change her mind and take the babies back—no questions asked. Fortunately, I was so sleep-deprived and busy that I did not pay too much attention to the passage of time. I did not sleep for more than an hour and a half at a time. Apparently, this is how some war criminals are tortured! Each twin gulped down eight bottles per day and so my daily rituals included sterilizing, preparing, and feeding sixteen bottles to the twins throughout the day and night while meeting the needs of a recently-adopted four-year old. Furthermore, coaxing sixteen burps each day took a lot of my time and energy. Our first and foremost concern was the welfare of all three of our children, and not the impending legal proceedings.

Even so, I felt some relief when I received a call that the four months had passed without any intervention from the birth mother. Now it was time to file the next round of adoption-related papers with the courts. In between appointments, very little action was required on our part. Whenever our lawyer called, we dutifully marched down to his office and signed the required papers. Then we went home and returned to parenting.

By this point in our adoption experiences, I was becoming immune to life-altering phone calls and so was hardly fazed when our lawyer's office called with our court date. The twins were already one year old, and we would become their legal parents. Until this point, we were their legal guardians and, as far as I was concerned, we were their parents from day one. But if the Quebec government needed us to say so in court, it was the least we could do to keep our family intact.

At least I felt confident that this court appearance would be easier than the one with our stern-faced Ukrainian judge. One similarity is that we needed to answer the big question—why did we want to adopt these children? In this case, it seemed like an odd question to answer, as we had no doubt that these babies, whom we'd been actively and exclusively parenting for a year, were already our own. However, we knew the importance of jumping through the required hoops and so answered all the questions thrown at us as honestly and completely as we could, without expressing any annoyance about their irrelevance.

Other than getting dressed up and going downtown, our court date was a day like any other. It began with making bottles and changing diapers and ended the same way. In between, though, something significant had taken place and the children were none the wiser. Without much fanfare, the courts declared us the legal parents of Matthew and Nicholas. We were thrilled! Our family was complete until, quite some time later, we adopted our beautiful, brown-eyed Chloe. By the way, Chloe is a six-pound Shih Tzu.

Afterword

We Are Family

This was not the end of our story but the beginning, as we began our life as a family with our three amazing children. I started this book during Katja's adoption. When we were blessed with Matt and Nick (as they now prefer to be called) as well, I knew I had to include their story in this book to complete our family puzzle. I was overloaded with the daily activities involved with raising a family of three children along with a professional career, and so our story had to wait until now to be shared.

Dave and I reflect on the fact that we never would have guessed we were meant to build our family in this way. We both assumed that our children would readily enter our lives whenever we planned to start our family. I would like to say that we instinctively knew to search the adoption route, as that would have made those years much easier. For us to complete our story, we had to be led down paths we did not expect. I am grateful that we looked down those paths that opened before us, instead of lamenting about the doors that seemed to close on us.

If you are considering an adoption but are worried that the

risks outweigh the benefits, I am here to tell you that any hard-ships we had to endure are forgotten. Well, they are not completely forgotten, or I would not be able to write and rework this book! Some pages were more difficult to write than others, as I can still feel the anxiety and pain that was prevalent when we had no way of knowing how the story would unfold. Nothing in life is a sure thing, but I do know that if adoption is meant for your family, you are truly blessed.

My sincere hope is that our story inspires you to achieve your family goals or any other goals of significance in your life. As your Coach, I will wrap up by reminding you of the lessons I learned along the way that transcend an adoption journey. First, I strongly encourage you to take the time to develop a compelling vision for your family, and then surround yourself with people who will support you in your journey. Do not let anyone deter you from creating the family of your dreams simply because they fail to see your vision before it is realized. Expect that you will be presented with obstacles, assume you will overcome them, and act accord-ingly. Sure, there may be some challenging situations you cannot control. However, if you keep making progress wherever you can, one step at a time, you will achieve more than if you anticipate failure. Don't forget to celebrate your successes along the way. To the extent possible, enjoy the journey. I wish you all the best!

Lightning Source UK Ltd.
Milton Keynes UK
UKHW010633040621
384928UK00001B/210